COLUMBIA COLLEGE CHICAGO

TELEVISION STANDARDS?:
IND

TELEVISION STANDARDS?:
INDECENCY, BOOZE
AND VIOLENCE

J.V. BARTON
EDITOR

Novinka Books
New York

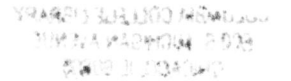

Copyright © 2005 by Novinka Books
An imprint of Nova Science Publishers, Inc.

All rights reserved. No part of this book may be reproduced, stored in a retrieval system or transmitted in any form or by any means: electronic, electrostatic, magnetic, tape, mechanical photocopying, recording or otherwise without the written permission of the Publisher.

For permission to use material from this book please contact us:
Telephone 631-231-7269; Fax 631-231-8175
Web Site: http://www.novapublishers.com

NOTICE TO THE READER

The Publisher has taken reasonable care in the preparation of this book, but makes no expressed or implied warranty of any kind and assumes no responsibility for any errors or omissions. No liability is assumed for incidental or consequential damages in connection with or arising out of information contained in this book. The Publisher shall not be liable for any special, consequential, or exemplary damages resulting, in whole or in part, from the readers' use of, or reliance upon, this material.

This publication is designed to provide accurate and authoritative information with regard to the subject matter covered herein. It is sold with the clear understanding that the Publisher is not engaged in rendering legal or any other professional services. If legal or any other expert assistance is required, the services of a competent person should be sought. FROM A DECLARATION OF PARTICIPANTS JOINTLY ADOPTED BY A COMMITTEE OF THE AMERICAN BAR ASSOCIATION AND A COMMITTEE OF PUBLISHERS.

Library of Congress Cataloging-in-Publication Data:
Available Upon Request

ISBN: 1-59454-033-0

Published by Nova Science Publishers, Inc. ✣ New York

CONTENTS

Chapter 1 Regulation of Broadcast Indecency:
Background and Legal Analysis 1
Angie A. Welborn and Henry Cohen

Chapter 2 V-Chip and TV Ratings:
Monitoring Children's Access to TV Programming 41
Patricia Moloney Figliola

Chapter 3 Obscenity and Indecency:
Constitutional Principles and Federal Statutes 59
Henry Cohen

Chapter 4 Obscenity, Child Pornography, and Indecency:
Recent Developments and Pending Issues 105
Henry Cohen

PREFACE

The Federal Communications Commission (FCC) has been bombarded with hundreds of thousands of complaints concerning the 2004 Super Bowl halftime show. Although the focal point of the complaints has been a public breast exposure, the complaints perhaps reflect the general outrage at a halftime show which has been described as a raunchy and disgraceful public display of indecency. The National Football League took a huge risk with its franchise presentation which has already reached over 100 million viewers. The FCC, however, is supposed to function as the guardian of what passes for a certain level of public decency and cultural acceptability. But has it been doing that or has it deteriorated to a little more than a back-water refuge for nepotism and industry fawning? This book presents media analyses of what the FCC is supposed to do – not what it does based on results.

Chapter 1

REGULATION OF BROADCAST INDECENCY: BACKGROUND AND LEGAL ANALYSIS*

Angie A. Welborn and Henry Cohen

ABSTRACT

Two prominent television events in the past two years placed increased attention on the FCC and its indecency regulations. The airing of the 2003 Golden Globe Awards and the subsequent ruling by the FCC's Enforcement Bureau, coupled with the controversy surrounding the 2004 Super Bowl halftime show, brought broadcast indecency to the forefront of the congressional agenda during the 108th Congress.

Several bills were introduced, but not enacted, in the 108th Congress to increase the penalties imposed for broadcast indecency and to prohibit the broadcast of certain words and phrases in any grammatical form. Similar legislation has been introduced in the 109th Congress. This report provides background on the two events in question, discusses the legal evolution of the FCC's indecency regulations, and provides an overview of how the current regulations have been applied and pending legislation. The final section of the

---

* Excerpted from CRS Report RL32222 dated March 30, 2005

report considers whether prohibiting the broadcast of "indecent" words regardless of context would violate the First Amendment.

INTRODUCTION

Two prominent television events in the past two years placed increased attention on the Federal Communications Commission (FCC) and its broadcast indecency regulations. [1] The airing of the 2003 Golden Globe Awards and the subsequent ruling of the FCC's Enforcement Bureau, coupled with the controversy surrounding the 2004 Super Bowl half-time show, have brought broadcast indecency to the forefront of the congressional agenda. During the 108th Congress, several bills were introduced to increase the penalties imposed for broadcast indecency and prohibit the broadcast of certain words and phrases though none of the legislation was enacted.

In addition, both the House and Senate held hearings on broadcast indecency.

Similar legislation has been introduced in the 109th Congress. This report provides background on the two events in question, discusses the legal evolution of the FCC's indecency regulations, and provides an overview of how the current regulations have been applied and pending legislation. The final section of the report considers whether prohibiting the broadcast of "indecent" words regardless of context would violate the First Amendment. [2]

BACKGROUND

On January 19, 2003, a number of broadcast television stations in various parts of the country aired the Golden Globe Awards. During the awards, the performer Bono, in response to winning an award, uttered the phrase "this is really, really f[***]ing brilliant." [3] In response to this utterance, the FCC received over 230 complaints alleging that the program was obscene or indecent, and requesting that the Commission impose sanctions on the licensees for the broadcast of the material in question. [4]

The Enforcement Bureau of the FCC issued a Memorandum Opinion and Order on October 3, 2003, denying the complaints and finding that the broadcast of the Golden Globe Awards including Bono's utterance did not violate federal restrictions regarding the broadcast of obscene and indecent material. [5] The Bureau dismissed the complaints primarily because the language in question did not describe or depict sexual or excretory activities or organs. The Bureau noted that while "the word 'f[***]ing' may be crude and offensive," it "did not describe sexual or excretory organs or activities. Rather, the performer used the word 'f[***]ing' as an adjective or expletive to emphasize an exclamation." [6] The Bureau added that in similar circumstances it "found that offensive language used as an insult rather than as a description of sexual or excretory activity or organs is not within the scope of the Commission's prohibition on indecent program content." [7]

The decision of the Enforcement Bureau was met with opposition from a number of organizations and Members of Congress, and an appeal was filed for review by the full Commission. FCC Chairman Michael Powell asked the full Commission to overturn the Enforcement Bureau's ruling. [8]

On March 18, 2004, the full Commission issued a *Memorandum Opinion and Order* granting the application for review and reversing the Enforcement Bureau's earlier opinion. [9] The Commission found that the broadcasts of the Golden Globe Awards violated 18 U.S.C. 1464, but declined to impose a forfeiture on the broadcast licensees because the Order reverses Commission precedent regarding the broadcast of the "F-word." This decision is discussed in detail below.

On February 1, 2004, CBS aired Super Bowl XXXVIII, with a half-time show produced by the MTV network. The show included performers singing and dancing provocatively, and ended with the exposure of the breast of one female performer.

The network received numerous complaints regarding the half-time performance and FCC Chairman Michael Powell initiated a formal investigation into the incident. [10] On September 22, 2004, the FCC released a *Notice of Apparent Liability for Forfeiture* finding that the airing of the Super Bowl halftime show "apparently violate[d] the federal restrictions regarding the broadcast of indecent material." [11] The *NAL* imposes a forfeiture in the aggregate amount of $550,000 on Viacom Inc., the licensee or ultimate parent of the licensees with regard to whom the complaint was filed. [12] This decision is discussed in detail below.

EVOLUTION OF THE FCC'S INDECENCY REGULATIONS

Title 18 of the United States Code makes it unlawful to utter "any obscene, indecent, or profane language by means of radio communication." [13] Violators of this provision are subject to fines or imprisonment of up to two years. The Federal Communications Commission has the authority to enforce this provision by forfeiture or revocation of license. [14] The Commission's authority to regulate material that is indecent, but not obscene, was upheld by the Supreme Court in *Federal Communications Commission v. Pacifica Foundation*. [15] In *Pacifica*, the Supreme Court affirmed the Commission's order regarding the airing of comedian George Carlin's "Filthy Words" monologue. [16] In that order, the Commission determined that the airing of the monologue, which contained certain words that "depicted sexual and excretory activities in a patently offensive manner," at a time "when children were undoubtedly in the audience" was indecent and prohibited by 18 U.S.C. § 1464. [17] Pursuant to the Court's decision, whether any such material is "patently offensive" is determined by "contemporary community standards for the broadcast medium." [18] The Court noted that indecency is "largely a function of context — it cannot be judged in the abstract." [19]

The Commission's order in the *Pacifica* case relied partially on a spectrum scarcity argument; i.e., that there is a scarcity of spectrum space so the government must license the use of such space in the public interest, and partially on "principles analogous to those found in the law of nuisance." [20] The Commission noted that public nuisance law generally aims to channel the offensive behavior rather than to prohibit it outright. For example, in the context of broadcast material, channeling would involve airing potentially offensive material at times when children are less likely to be in the audience. In 1987, the Commission rejected the spectrum scarcity argument as a sufficient basis for its regulation of broadcast indecency, but noted that it would continue to rely upon the validity of the public nuisance rationale, including channeling of potentially objectionable material. [21] However, in its 1987 order, the Commission also stated that channeling based on a specific time of day was no longer a sufficient means to ensure that children were not in the audience when indecent material aired and warned licensees that indecent material aired after 10 p.m. would be actionable. [22] The Commission further clarified its earlier *Pacifica* order, noting that indecent language was not strictly limited to the seven words at issue in the original broadcast in question, and that repeated use of those words was not necessary to find that material in question was indecent. [23]

The Commission's 1987 orders were challenged by parties alleging that the Commission had changed its indecency standard and that the new standard was unconstitutional. In *Action for Children's Television v. Federal Communications Commission (ACT I)*, the United States Court of Appeals for the District of Columbia Circuit upheld the standard used by the Commission to determine whether broadcast material was indecent, but it vacated the Commission's order with respect to the channeling of indecent material for redetermination "after a full and fair hearing of the times at which indecent material may be broadcast." [24]

Following the court's decision in *Action for Children's Television (ACT I)*, a rider to the Commerce, Justice, State FY89 Appropriations Act required the FCC to promulgate regulations to ban indecent broadcasts 24 hours a day. [25] The Commission followed the congressional mandate and promulgated regulations prohibiting all broadcasts of indecent material. [26] The new regulations were challenged, and the United States Court of Appeals for the District of Columbia Circuit vacated the Commission's order. [27] In so doing, the court noted that in *ACT I* it held that Commission "must identify some reasonable period of time during which indecent material may be broadcast," thus precluding a ban on such broadcasts at all times. [28]

In 1992, Congress enacted the Public Telecommunications Act of 1992, which required the FCC to promulgate regulations to prohibit the broadcasting of indecent material from 6 a.m. to midnight, except for broadcasts by public radio and television stations that go off the air at or before midnight, in which case such stations may broadcast indecent material beginning at 10 p.m. [29] The Commission promulgated regulations as mandated in the act. [30] The new regulations were challenged, and a three-judge panel of the United States Court of Appeals for the District of Columbia Circuit subsequently vacated the Commission's order implementing the act and held the underlying statute unconstitutional. [31] In its order implementing the act, the FCC set forth three goals to justify the regulations: (1) ensuring that parents have an opportunity to supervise their children's listening and viewing of over-the-air broadcasts; (2) ensuring the well being of minors regardless of supervision; and (3) protecting the right of all members of the public to be free of indecent material in the privacy of their homes. [32] The court rejected the third justification as "insufficient to support a restriction on the broadcasting of constitutionally protected indecent material," but accepted the first two as compelling interests. [33]

Despite the finding of compelling interests in the first two, the court found that both Congress and the FCC had failed "to tailor their efforts to advance these interests in a sufficiently narrow way to meet constitutional standards." [34]

Following the decision of the three-judge panel, the Commission requested a rehearing *en banc*. [35] The case was reheard on October 19, 1994, and, on June 30, 1995, the full court of appeals held the statute unconstitutional insofar as it prohibited the broadcast of indecent material between the hours of 10 p.m. and midnight on nonpublic stations. [36] In so doing, the court held that while the channeling of indecent broadcasts between midnight and 6 a.m. "would not unduly burden the First Amendment," the distinction drawn by Congress between public and non-public broadcasters "bears no apparent relationship to the compelling government interests that [the restrictions] are intended to serve." [37] The court remanded the regulations to the FCC with instructions to modify the regulations to permit the broadcast of indecent material on all stations between 10 p.m and 6 a.m.

CURRENT REGULATIONS AND ANALYSIS

Following the decision in *ACT III*, the Commission modified its indecency regulations to prohibit the broadcast any material which is indecent on any day between 6 a.m. and 10 p.m. [38] The newly modified regulations became effective August 28, 1995. [39] These regulations have been enforced primarily with respect to radio broadcasts and thus have been applied to indecent language rather than to images. [40] Broadcasts deemed indecent are subject to a forfeiture of up to $32,500 per violation. [41] Recently, the FCC started considering each utterance of an indecent word as a separate violation, rather than viewing the entire program as a single violation, which could lead to fines in excess of $32,500. [42]

To determine whether broadcast material is in fact indecent, the Commission must make two fundamental determinations: (1) that the material alleged to be indecent falls within the subject matter scope of the definition of indecency — the material in question must describe or depict sexual or excretory organs or activities; and (2) that the broadcast is patently offensive as measured by contemporary community standards for the broadcast medium. [43] If the material in question does not fall within the subject matter scope of the indecency definition, [44] or if the broadcast occurred during the "safe harbor" hours (between 10 p.m. and 6 a.m.), the complaint is usually dismissed. [45] However, if the Commission determines that the complaint meets the subject matter requirements and was aired outside the "safe harbor" hours, the broadcast in question is evaluated for patent offensiveness. [46] The Commission notes that in determining whether material is patently offensive, the full context is very important, and that such determinations are highly fact-specific.

The Commission has identified three factors that have been significant in recent decisions in determining whether broadcast material is patently offensive:

> (1) the explicitness or graphic nature of the description or depiction of sexual or excretory organs or activities; (2) whether the material dwells on or repeats at length descriptions of sexual or excretory organs or activities; (3) whether the material appears to pander or is used to titillate, or whether the material appears to have been presented for its shock value. [47]

An overview and analysis of cases addressing each of these factors follows.

Explicitness or Graphic Nature of Material

Generally, the more explicit or graphic the description or depiction, the greater the likelihood that the material will be deemed patently offensive and therefore indecent. For example, the Commission imposed a forfeiture on a university radio station for airing a rap song that included a line depicting anal intercourse. [48] In that case, the Commission determined that the song described sexual activities in graphic terms that were patently offensive and therefore indecent. Since the song was broadcast in the mid-afternoon, there was a reasonable risk that children were in the audience, thus giving rise to the Commission's action. [49]

Broadcasts need not be as graphic as the song in the above case to give rise to the imposition of an FCC forfeiture. Broadcasts consisting of double entendres or innuendos may also be deemed indecent if the "sexual or excretory import is unmistakable." [50] The FCC issued a notice of apparent liability and imposed a forfeiture on several stations for airing a song that included the following lines: "I whipped out my Whopper and whispered, Hey, Sweettart, how'd you like to Crunch on my Big Hunk for a Million Dollar Bar? Well, she immediately went down on my Tootsie Roll and you know, it was like pure Almond Joy." [51] The Commission determined that the material was indecent even though it used candy bar names to substitute for sexual activities. In one notice concerning the broadcast of the song, the Commission stated that "[w]hile the passages arguably consist of double entendre and indirect references, the language used in each passage was understandable and clearly capable of specific sexual meaning and, because of the context, the sexual import was inescapable." [52] The nature of the lyrics, coupled with the fact that the song aired between 6 a.m. and 10 a.m., gave rise to the imposition of a forfeiture.

Dwelling or Repetition of Potentially Offensive Material

Repetition of and persistent focus on a sexual or excretory activity could "exacerbate the potential offensiveness of broadcasts." [53] For example, the FCC issued a notice of apparent liability and imposed a forfeiture on a radio station that broadcast an extensive discussion of flatulence and defecation by radio personality "Bubba, the Love Sponge." [54] Though the broadcast did not contain any expletives, the Commission found that the material dwelt on excretory activities and therefore was patently offensive.

While repetition can increase the likelihood that references to sexual or excretory activities are deemed indecent, where such references have been made in passing or are fleeting in nature, the Commission has found that the reference was not indecent even when profanity has been used. [55] For example, the Commission determined that the following phrase — "The hell I did, I drove mother-f[***]er, oh." — uttered by an announcer during a radio morning show, was not indecent. [56] The Commission declined to take action regarding the broadcast because it contained only a "fleeting and isolated utterance . . . within the context of live and spontaneous programming." [57] Certain fleeting references may, however, be found indecent where other factors contribute to the broadcast's patent offensiveness. For example, the Commission has imposed forfeitures on stations for airing jokes that refer to sexual activities with children. [58]

Pandering or Titillating Nature of Material

In determining whether broadcast material is indecent, the Commission also looks to the purpose for which the material is being presented. Indecency findings generally involve material that is presented in a pandering or titillating nature, or material that is presented for the shock value of its language. For example, the Commission deemed a radio call-in survey about oral sex to be indecent based in part on the fact that the material was presented in a pandering and titillating manner. [59]

Whether a broadcast is presented in a pandering or titillating manner depends on the context in which the potentially indecent material is presented. Explicit images or graphic language does not necessarily mean that the broadcast is being presented in a pandering or titillating manner. For example, the Commission declined to impose a forfeiture on a television station for airing portions of a high school sex education class that included the use of "sex organ models to demonstrate the use of various birth control devices." [60] In dismissing the complaint, the Commission held that "[a]lthough the program dealt with sexual issues, the material presented was clinical or instructional in nature and not presented in a pandering, titillating, or vulgar manner." [61]

GOLDEN GLOBE AWARDS DECISION

As noted above, on March 18, 2004, the Federal Communications Commission overturned an earlier decision by the Commission's Enforcement Bureau regarding the broadcast of the word "f[***]ing" during the 2003 Golden Globe Awards. In the earlier decision, the Enforcement Bureau had found that the broadcast of the program including the utterance did not violate federal restrictions regarding the broadcast of obscene and indecent material. [62] The Bureau dismissed the complaints primarily because the language in question did not describe or depict sexual or excretory activities or organs.

In its March 18 *Memorandum Opinion and Order*, the full Commission concluded that the broadcast of the Golden Globe Awards did include material that violated prohibitions on the broadcast of indecent and profane material. [63] In reversing the Bureau, the Commission determined that the "phrase at issue is within the scope of our indecency definition because it does depict or describe sexual activities." [64] Although the Commission "recognize[d] NBC's argument that the 'FWord' here was used 'as an intensifier,'" it nevertheless concluded that, "given the core meaning of the 'F-Word,' any use of that word or a variation, in any context, inherently has a sexual connotation, and therefore falls within the first prong of our indecency definition." [65]

Upon finding that the phrase in question fell within the first prong of the definition of "indecency," the Commission turned to the question of whether the broadcast was patently offensive under contemporary community standards for the broadcast medium. The Commission determined that the broadcast was patently offensive, noting that "[t]he 'F-Word' is one of the most vulgar, graphic and explicit descriptions of sexual activity in the English language," and that "[t]he use of the 'FWord' here, on a nationally telecast awards ceremony, was shocking and gratuitous." [66] The Commission also rejected "prior Commission and staff action [that] have indicated that isolated or fleeting broadcasts of the 'F-Word' such as that here are not indecent or would not be acted upon," concluding "that any such interpretation is no longer good law." [67] The Commission further clarified its position, stating "that the mere fact that specific words or phrases are not sustained or repeated does not mandate a finding that material that is otherwise patently offensive to the broadcast medium is not indecent." [68]

In addition to the determination that the utterance of the word "f[***]ing" during the Golden Globe Awards was indecent, the Commission also found, as an independent ground for its decision, that use of the word was "profane" in violation of 18 U.S.C. 1464. [69] In making this determination, the Commission cited dictionary definitions of "profanity" as "'vulgar, irreverent, or coarse language,'" [70] and a Seventh Circuit opinion stating that "profanity" is "'construable as denoting certain of those personally reviling epithets naturally tending to provoke violent resentment or denoting language so grossly offensive to members of the public who actually hear it as to amount to a nuisance.'" [71] The Commission acknowledged that its limited case law regarding profane speech has focused on profanity in the context of blasphemy, but stated that it would no longer limit its definition of profane speech in such manner. Pursuant to its adoption of this new definition of "profane," the Commission stated that, depending on the context, the "'F-Word' and those words (or variants thereof) that are as highly offensive as the 'F-Word'" would be considered "profane" if broadcast between 6 a.m. and 10 p.m. [72] The Commission noted that other words would be considered on a case-by-case basis.

SUPER BOWL HALFTIME SHOW DECISION

As noted above, on September 22, 2004, the FCC released a *Notice of Apparent Liability for Forfeiture* imposing a $550,000 forfeiture on several Viacom-owned CBS affiliates for the broadcast of the Super Bowl XXXVIII halftime show on February 1, 2004, in which a performer's breast was exposed. [73] The Commission determined that the show, which was aired at approximately 8:30 p.m. Eastern Standard Time, violated its restrictions on the broadcast of indecent material.

In its analysis, the Commission determined that since the broadcast included a performance that culminated in "on-camera partial nudity," and thus satisfied the first part of the indecency analysis, further scrutiny was warranted to determine whether the broadcast was "patently offensive as measured by contemporary community standards for the broadcast medium." [74] The Commission found that the performance in question was "both explicit and graphic," and rejected the licensees' contention that since the exposure was fleeting, lasting only 19/32 of a second, it should not be deemed indecent. [75] In determining whether the material in question was intended to "pander to, titillate and shock the viewing audience," the Commission noted that the performer's breast was exposed after another performer sang, "gonna have you naked by the end of this song." [76] The Commission found that the song lyrics, coupled with simulated sexual activities during the performance and the exposure of the breast, indicated that the purpose of the performance was to pander to, titillate and shock the audience, and the fact that the actual exposure of the breast was brief, as noted above, was not dispositive. [77]

The Commission ordered each Viacom-owned CBS affiliate to pay the statutory maximum forfeiture of $27,500 for the broadcast, for a total forfeiture of $550,000.

The forfeiture was imposed on the Viacom-owned affiliates because of Viacom's participation in and planning of the Super Bowl halftime show with MTV networks, another Viacom subsidiary. [78]

Following the issuance of the *Notice of Apparent Liability for Forfeiture*, the affiliates are "afforded a reasonable period of time (usually 30 days from the date of the notice) to show, in writing, why a forfeiture penalty should not be imposed or should be reduced, or to pay the forfeiture." [79] CBS filed an opposition to the Notice of Apparent Liability on November 5, 2004. The opposition challenged the forfeiture on various grounds, including that the test for indecency was not met and that the forfeiture violates the First Amendment. The Commission may now issue an order cancelling or reducing the proposed forfeiture, or it may require that the original amount be paid in full by a certain date. [80] This order, constituting a final agency action, may subsequently be appealed in federal court. [81]

OTHER RECENT ENFORCEMENT ACTIONS

In addition to the Commission's forfeiture proceedings discussed above, the Commission has recently imposed forfeitures on a number of radio stations for broadcast indecency. [82] We now discuss two of its recent high-profile actions.

Infinity Broadcasting

On October 2, 2003, the Commission issued a *Notice of Apparent Liability* to Infinity Broadcasting for airing portions of the "Opie & Anthony Show" during which the hosts conducted a contest entitled "Sex for Sam" which involved couples having sex in certain "risky" locations throughout New York City in an effort to win a trip. [83] The couples, accompanied by a station employee, were to have sex in as many of the designated locations as possible. They were assigned points based on the nature of the location and the activities in which they engaged. The station aired discussions between the hosts of the show and the station employee accompanying the couples which consisted of descriptions of the sexual activities of the participating couples and the locations in which they engaged in sexual activities. One discussion involved an description of a couple apparently engaging in sexual activities in St. Patrick's Cathedral.

The Commission determined that the broadcast made "graphic and explicit references to sexual and excretory organs and activity" despite the fact that colloquial terms, rather than explicit or graphic terms, were used in the descriptions. The Commission found that "[t]o the extent that the colloquial terms that the participants used to describe organs and activities could be described as innuendo rather than as direct references, they are nonetheless sufficient to render the material actionably indecent because the 'sexual [and] excretory import' of those references was 'unmistakable.'" [84] The Commission also found that the hosts of the show "dwelled at length on and referred repeatedly to sexual or excretory activities and organs," and that "the descriptions of sexual and excretory activity and organs were not in any way isolated and fleeting." [85]

On November 23, 2004, the FCC entered into a consent decree with Infinity regarding the Opie & Anthony *NAL*. [86] Pursuant to the decree, Infinity, a subsidiary of Viacom, agreed to make a voluntary contribution to the United States Treasury in the amount of $3.5 million and to adopt a company-wide compliance plan for the purpose of preventing the broadcast of indecent material. As part of the companywide plan, Viacom agreed to install delay systems to edit "potentially problematic" live programming and to conduct training with respect to indecency regulations for all of its on-air talent and employees who participate in programming decisions.

Clear Channel Broadcasting

On January 27, 2004, the Commission issued a *Notice of Apparent Liability* to Clear Channel Broadcasting for repeated airings of the "Bubba, the Love Sponge" program which included indecent material. [87]

The Commission found that all the broadcasts in question involved "conversations about such things as oral sex, penises, testicles, masturbation, intercourse, orgasms and breasts." [88] The Commission determined that each of the broadcasts in question contained "sufficiently graphic and explicit references," which were generally repeated throughout the broadcast in a pandering and titillating manner.

In one broadcast, the station aired a segment involving skits in which the voices of purported cartoon characters talk about drugs and sex. [89] The skits were inserted between advertisements for Cartoon Network's Friday-night cartoons. The Commission determined that "the use of cartoon characters in such a sexually explicit manner during hours of the day when children are likely to be listening is shocking and makes this segment patently offensive." [90] The Commission also cited the "calculated and callous nature of the stations' decision to impose this predictably offensive material upon young, vulnerable listeners" as "weighing heavily" in its determination. [91]

On April 8, 2004, the Commission released another *Notice of Apparent Liability* against Clear Channel Communications for airing allegedly indecent material during the "Howard Stern Show." [92] For the first time, the Commission sought to impose separate statutory maximum forfeitures for each indecent utterance during the program in question, rather than imposing a single fine for the entire program. [93]

The Commission entered into a consent decree with Clear Channel on June 9, 2004. The decree requires Clear Channel to make a "voluntary contribution" of $1.75 million to the United States Treasury and outlines "a company-wide compliance plan for the purpose of preventing the broadcast over radio or television of material violative of the indecency laws." [94] As part of the compliance plan, Clear Channel will "conduct training on obscenity and indecency for all on-air talent and employees who materially participate in programming decisions, which will include tutorials regarding material that the FCC does not permit broadcasters to air." [95] The plan also requires Clear Chanel to suspend any employee accused of airing, or who materially participates in the decision to air, obscene or indecent material while an investigation is conducted following the issuance of a *Notice of Apparent Liability*. Such employees will be terminated without delay if the *NAL* results in enforcement action by the FCC.

CONGRESSIONAL RESPONSE

108th Congress

Several bills addressing broadcast indecency were introduced during the 108th Congress, but none were enacted.

In response to the FCC's initial decision regarding the Golden Globe Awards broadcast, Representative Ose introduced legislation that would have amended section 1464 of title 18 to define "profane," as used in that section, to include any use of eight specific words or phrases, in any grammatical form. [96]

Legislation was also introduced, by Representative Upton, that would have increased the FCC's penalties for broadcasting obscene, indecent, and profane language. H.R. 3717, 108th Congress, would have increased the penalties to $275,000 for each violation or each day of a continuing violation, with the total amount assessed for any continuing violation not to exceed $3 million for any single act or failure to act. The bill specifically mentioned obscene, indecent, and profane language, but did not appear to impose the increased penalties for broadcast images that were deemed indecent.

On March 3, 2004, the House Committee on Energy and Commerce held a full-committee markup of H.R. 3717. The Committee approved an amendment in the nature of a substitute and ordered the bill to be reported to the full House. [97] The amendment would have increased the maximum penalty for the broadcast of indecent material to $500,000 for each violation with no aggregate maximum. Under the amendment, the increased forfeiture penalties could have also been imposed on nonlicensees, such as individuals who utter obscene, indecent, or profane material.

In determining the appropriate amount of the forfeiture, the bill directed the Commission to consider a number of factors, including whether the material in question was live or recorded, scripted or unscripted, and the size of the viewing audience. The Commission would have been required to act on allegations of broadcast indecency within 180 days after the receipt of the allegation.

In addition to the increased penalties, the legislation also would have provided additional nonmonetary penalties for the broadcast of indecent material. If the Commission determined that a licensee had broadcast obscene, indecent, or profane material, the Commission would have been able to require the licensee to broadcast public service announcements that serve the educational and informational needs of children, and such announcements could have been required to reach an audience that was up to five times the size of the audience that was estimated to have been reached by the obscene, indecent, or profane material. The legislation also directed the Commission to take into consideration whether the broadcast of obscene, indecent, or profane material demonstrated a lack of character or other qualifications to operate a station. The broadcast of such material would have also been considered a serious violation for purposes of license renewal determinations. Finally, if during the term of the license, a broadcast licensee was the subject of three or more proceedings regarding violations of indecency prohibitions, the Commission would have been required to commence a proceeding to consider whether the license should be revoked.

The House passed H.R. 3717 on March 11, 2004, with two additional amendments. [98] The first amendment would have preserved a licensee's right to appeal a forfeiture before it could have been considered during a license application or renewal proceeding, or used in a license revocation proceeding initiated after the licensee's third indecency violation. The second amendment approved by the House would have required the GAO to study the number of indecency complaints received by the FCC and the number of those complaints that result in final agency action by the Commission; the amount of time taken by the Commission to respond to a complaint; the mechanisms established by the Commission to receive, investigate, and respond to complaints; and whether complainants to the Commission are adequately informed by the Commission of the responses to their complaints. The amendment gave GAO one year to complete the study and report to Congress on its findings.

On February 9, 2004, Senator Brownback introduced S. 2056, which was virtually identical to H.R. 3717, as introduced. On March 9, 2004, the Senate Committee on Commerce, Science and Transportation held a full committee markup of the bill, and ordered the bill to be reported favorably with amendments. [99] As reported, the bill included a number of provisions similar to those in H.R. 3717.

Both bills would have increased forfeiture amounts for broadcast indecency, but unlike the House bill, which included an initial increase to $500,000 per violation, the Senate bill would have provided for an initial increase to $275,000 per violation, with additional increases, up to $500,000, for subsequent violations. Penalties could have been doubled if the Commission determined that certain aggravating factors were met. Like the House bill, the Senate bill included a provision that would have required the FCC to commence a license revocation hearing if a broadcast licensee had been the subject of three proceedings regarding indecency violations. The Senate bill would have also required the Commission to act on any allegations of broadcast indecency within 270 days.

Additional amendments to S. 2056 would have directed the Commission to consider a broadcaster's ability to pay forfeitures based on factors such as revenues and market size when determining the amount of the forfeiture, and would have invalidated the FCC's media ownership rules pending a GAO review of the relationship between horizontal and vertical consolidation of media companies and violations of indecency prohibitions. [100]

Another Senate bill aimed at increasing penalties for broadcast indecency was introduced by Senator Miller on March 1, 2004. S. 2147 would have allowed the Commission to impose a forfeiture of "25 cents times the number of individuals who witnessed or heard the broadcast as determined by a viewership rating service selected by the Commission" for the broadcast of obscene, indecent, or profane language. The forfeiture could have been imposed on broadcast licensees, any applicant for a broadcast license, or any other company or individual that had participated in the broadcast, including producers, general managers, performers, and networks.

On June 22, 2004, the Senate approved an amendment to the National Defense Authorization Act (S. 2400) which included provisions similar to those in S. 2056, as reported by the Senate Commerce, Science, and Transportation Committee on March 9, 2004. The amendment would have increased the maximum forfeiture imposed by the FCC to $275,000 per violation, with a cap of $3 million for a continuing violation. [101] The Senate's amendment to the National Defense Authorization Act was not adopted by the conference committee and was not included in the conference report as approved by both the House and Senate on October 9, 2004. [102]

In addition, S. 1264, 108th Congress, the FCC Reauthorization Act of 2003, as reported by the Committee on Commerce on September 3, 2003 (prior to the FCC Enforcement Bureau's decision regarding the Golden Globe Awards broadcast), would have, in section 11, required that "the broadcast of obscene or indecent matter from more than 1 individual during the same program" be considered separate violations, and that the FCC, unless it determined it not to be in the public interest, revoke the station license or construction permit of any broadcast station licensee or permittee that violates 18 U.S.C. § 1464.

None of the above indecency provisions was enacted into law.

Finally, several resolutions were introduced to express disapproval of the FCC Enforcement Bureau's decision regarding the Golden Globe Awards broadcast: H.Res. 482, H.Res. 500, and S.Res. 283, which the Senate passed on December 9, 2003. None of the House resolutions were acted upon.

109th Congress

Legislation addressing broadcast indecency has been introduced during the 109th Congress. In general, these bills are similar to legislation introduced during the 108th Congress.

H.R. 310, 109th Congress, entitled the Broadcast Decency Enforcement Act of 2005, would increase penalties for the broadcast of obscene, indecent, or profane material to a maximum of $500,000 for each violation, and would provide penalties for nonlicensees, such as artists and performers. [103] In addition to the increased forfeiture amount, the Federal Communications Commission would be able to require licensees to broadcast public service announcements that serve the educational and informational needs of children and require such announcements to reach an audience up to five times greater than the size of the audience that is estimated to have been reached by the obscene, indecent or profane broadcast. Also, any violation of the Commission's indecency regulations could be considered when determining whether to grant or renew a broadcast license, and three or more indecency violations would trigger a license revocation proceeding. The legislation would also require the Commission to act upon allegations of indecency within 180 days of the receipt of the allegation.

On February 9, 2005, the House Committee on Energy and Commerce reported H.R. 310 favorably without amendment. The House passed H.R. 310 on February 16, with one amendment. The amendment made several nonsubstantive technical changes and added a section requiring the FCC to revise its policy statement regarding broadcast indecency within nine months of the date of enactment of the legislation and at least once every three years thereafter. [104]

H.R. 1420, 109th Congress, entitled the Families for ED Advertising Decency Act, would require the Federal Communications Commission to revise its interpretations of, and enforcement policies concerning the broadcast of indecent material to treat as indecent any advertisement for a medication for the treatment of erectile dysfunction, thus prohibiting the airing of such advertisements between the hours of 6 a.m. and 10 p.m.

H.R. 1440, 109th Congress, entitled the Stamp Out Censorship Act of 2005, would prohibit the Federal Communications Commission from imposing forfeitures for indecency on nonbroadcast programming.

S. 193, 109th Congress, also entitled the Broadcast Decency Enforcement Act of 2005, would increase the maximum forfeiture for the broadcast of obscene, indecent, or profane material to $325,000 for each violation, with a cap of $3,000,000 for any single act or failure to act.

S. 616, 109th Congress, entitled the Indecent and Gratuitous and Excessively Violent Programming Control Act of 2005, would, *inter alia*, require the Federal Communications Commission to study the effectiveness of measures used by multichannel video programming distributors to protect children from exposure to indecent and violent programming. If the Commission were to determine that such measures were not effective, the legislation directs the Commission to initiate a rulemaking proceeding to adopt measures to protect children from indecent programming carried by multichannel video programming distributors during the hours when children are reasonably likely to be a substantial portion of the television audience. The bill would also increase the penalty for the broadcast of obscene, indecent, or profane language or images to $500,000, with a maximum forfeiture for any violations occurring in a given 24-hour period set at $3,000,000. The Commission would be required to take certain factors into consideration when imposing a forfeiture, and would be required to conduct public hearings or forums prior to the imposition of a forfeiture. Additionally, broadcast licensees would be allowed to preempt programming from a network organization that it deems obscene, and all television and radio broadcast licensees and multichannel video programming distributors would be required to provide a warning of the specific content of each recorded or scripted program it broadcasts.

WOULD PROHIBITING THE BROADCAST OF "INDECENT" WORDS REGARDLESS OF CONTEXT VIOLATE THE FIRST AMENDMENT?

In 1978, in *Federal Communications Commission v. Pacifica Foundation*, the Supreme Court upheld, against a First Amendment challenge, an action that FCC took against a radio station for broadcasting a recording of George Carlin's "Filthy Words" monologue at 2 p.m. [105] The Court has not decided a case on the issue of "indecent" speech on broadcast radio or television since then, but it did cite *Pacifica* with approval in 1997, when, in *Reno v. ACLU*, it contrasted regulation of the broadcast media with regulation of the Internet. [106] Nevertheless, the Court in *Reno* did not *hold* that *Pacifica* remains good law, and arguments have been made that the proliferation of cable television channels has rendered archaic *Pacifica*'s denial of full First Amendment rights to broadcast media.

Even if *Pacifica* remains valid in this respect, *Pacifica* did not hold that the First Amendment permits the ban either of an occasional expletive on broadcast media, or of programs that would not be likely to attract youthful audiences, even if such programs contain "indecent" language. On these points, Justice Stevens wrote for the Court in *Pacifica*:

> It is appropriate, in conclusion, to emphasize the narrowness of our holding. This case does not involve a two-way radio conversation between a cab driver and a dispatcher, or a telecast of an Elizabethan comedy. We have not decided that an occasional expletive in either setting would justify any sanction. . . . The time of day was emphasized by the Commission. The content of the program in which the language is used will also affect the composition of the audience. . . . [107]

In a footnote to the last sentence of this quotation, the Court added: "Even a prime-time recitation of Geoffrey Chaucer's Miller's Tale would not be likely to command the attention of many children. . . ." [108] At the same time, Justice Stevens acknowledged that the Carlin monologue has political content: "The monologue does present a point of view; it attempts to show that the words it uses are 'harmless' and that our attitudes toward them are 'essentially silly.' The Commission objects, [however,] not to this point of view, but to the way in which it is expressed." [109] The Court commented: "If there were any reason to believe that the Commission's characterization of the Carlin monologue as offensive could be traced to its political content

— or even to the fact that it satirized contemporary attitudes about four-letter words — First Amendment protection might be required." [110]

There appears to be some tension between this comment and the Court's remark about Chaucer, as any attempt to censor Chaucer would presumably also be based not on its ideas but on the way its ideas are expressed. But, as noted above, the Court's remark about Chaucer was a footnote to its comment that "[t]he content of the program in which the language is used will also affect the composition of the audience. . . ." Therefore, the difference that Justice Stevens apparently perceived between Chaucer and Carlin was that, even if both have literary, artistic, or political value, only the latter would be likely to attract a youthful audience. Arguably, then, *Pacifica* would permit the censorship, during certain hours, of the broadcast even of works of art that are likely to attract a youthful audience. [111]

If so, this would be contrary to the Court's opposition, in other contexts, to the censorship of works of art. The Court has held that even "materials [that] depict or describe patently offensive 'hard core' sexual conduct," which would otherwise be obscene, may not be prohibited if they have "serious literary, artistic, political, or scientific value." [112] In addition, the "harmful to minors" statutes of the sort that the Supreme Court upheld in *Ginsberg v. New York* generally define "harmful to minors" to parallel the Supreme Court's definition of "obscenity," and thus prohibit distributing to minors only material that lacks serious value for minors. [113] This suggests that, if the FCC or Congress prohibited the broadcast during certain hours of "indecent" words regardless of context, the Court might be troubled by the prohibition's application to works with serious value, even though *Pacifica* allowed the censorship of Carlin's monologue, despite its apparently having serious value.

Yet, as noted, Justice Stevens' expressed a distinction in *Pacifica* between a point of view and the way in which it is expressed, and, though a majority of the justices did not join the part of the opinion that drew this distinction, a majority of the justices, by concurring in *Pacifica*'s holding, indicated that the political (or literary or artistic) content of Carlin's monologue did not prevent its censorship during certain hours on broadcast radio and television. Therefore, it appears that, in deciding the constitutionality of an FCC or a congressional action prohibiting the broadcasting, during certain hours, of material with "indecent" words, the Court might be troubled by its application to works with serious value only if those works would, like Chaucer's, not likely attract a substantial youthful audience.

In sum, the Court did not hold that the FCC could prohibit an occasional expletive, and did not hold that the FCC could prohibit offensive words in programs — even prime-time programs — that children would be unlikely to watch or listen to. The Court did not hold that the FCC could *not* take these actions, as the question whether it could was not before the Court. But the Court's language quoted above renders *Pacifica* of uncertain precedential value in deciding whether a ban, during certain hours, on the broadcast of "indecent" words regardless of context would be constitutional.

In the "Filthy Words" monologue, as the Supreme Court described it, George Carlin "began by referring to his thoughts about 'the words you couldn't say on the public, ah, airwaves, um, the ones you definitely wouldn't say, ever.' He proceeded to list those words and repeat them over and over in a variety of colloquialisms." The FCC, at the time, used essentially the same standard for "indecent" that it uses today: "[T]he concept of 'indecent' is intimately connected with the exposure of children to language that describes, in terms patently offensive as measured by contemporary community standards for the broadcast medium, sexual or excretory activities and organs. . . ." [114]

Most of Carlin's uses of the "filthy words," it appears from reading his monologue, which is included as an appendix to the Court's opinion, seem designed to show the words' multiple uses, apart from describing sexual or excretory activities or organs. Nevertheless, "the Commission concluded that certain words depicted sexual or excretory activities in a patently offensive manner. . . ." [115] Therefore, one might argue that, even if, under *Pacifica*, the First Amendment does not protect, during certain hours, the use on broadcast media of words that depict sexual or excretory activities in a patently offensive manner, it nevertheless might protect the use of those same words "as an adjective or expletive to emphasize an exclamation" (to quote the FCC Enforcement Bureau's opinion in the Bono case).

A counterargument might be that, in *Pacifica*, the Court noted that "the normal definition of 'indecent' merely refers to nonconformance with accepted standards of morality." [116] This suggests the possibility that the Court would have ruled the same way in *Pacifica* if the FCC had defined "indecent" loosely enough to include the use of a patently offensive word "as an adjective or expletive to emphasize an exclamation." But this is speculative, as the Court did not so rule. Further, as noted above, Court emphasized the narrowness of its holding, noting that it had "not decided that an occasional expletive . . . would justify any sanction. . . ." On what basis did the Court in *Pacifica* find that the FCC's action did not violate the First Amendment? In Part IV-C of opinion, which was joined by a majority of the justices, Justice Stevens wrote:

[O]f all forms of communication, it is broadcasting that has received the most limited First Amendment protection. Thus, although other speakers cannot be licensed except under laws that carefully define and narrow official discretion, a broadcaster may be deprived of his license and his forum if the Commission decides that such an action would serve "the public interest, convenience, and necessity." Similarly, although the First Amendment protects newspaper publishers from being required to print the replies of those whom they criticize, *Miami Herald Publishing Co. v. Tornillo*, 418 U.S. 241, it affords no such protection to broadcasters; on the contrary, they must give free time to the victims of their criticism. *Red Lion Broadcasting Co. v. FCC*, 395 U.S. 367.

The reasons for these distinctions are complex, but two have relevance to the present case. First, the broadcast media have established a uniquely pervasive presence in the lives of all Americans. Patently offensive, indecent material presented over the airwaves confronts the citizen, not only in public, but in the privacy of the home, where the individual's right to be left alone plainly outweighs the First Amendment rights of an intruder. *Rowan v. Post Office Dept.*, 397 U.S. 728. . . . To say that one may avoid further offense by turning off the radio when he hears indecent language is like saying that the remedy for an assault is to run away after the first blow.

Second, broadcasting is uniquely accessible to children, even those too young to read. . . . Bookstores and motion picture theaters . . . may be prohibited from making indecent material available to children. We held in *Ginsberg v. New York*, 390 U.S. 629, that the government's interest in the "well-being of its youth" and in supporting "parents' claim to authority in their own household" justified the regulation of otherwise protected expression. . . . [117]

In sum, the Court held that, on broadcast radio and television, during certain times of day, certain material may be prohibited because (1) it is patently offensive and indecent, and (2) it threatens the well-being of minors and their parents' authority in their own household. This raises the question of the extent to which the Court continues to allow the government (1) to treat broadcast media differently from other media, and (2) to censor speech on the ground that it is patently offensive and indecent, or threatens the well-being of minors and their parents' authority in their own household.

Broadcast Media

In *Red Lion Broadcasting Co. v. FCC*, which the Court cited in the above quotation from *Pacifica*, the Court upheld the FCC's "fairness doctrine," which "imposed on radio and television broadcasters the requirement that discussion of public issues be presented on broadcast stations, and that each side of those issues must be given fair coverage." [118] The reason that the Court upheld the imposition of the fairness doctrine on broadcast media, though it would not uphold its imposition on print media, is that "[w]here there are substantially more individuals who want to broadcast than there are frequencies to allocate, it is idle to posit an unabridgeable First Amendment right to broadcast comparable to the right of every individual to speak, write, or publish." [119] "Licenses to broadcast," the Court added, "do not confer ownership of designated frequencies, but only the temporary privilege of using them. 47 U.S.C. § 301. Unless renewed, they expire within three years. 47 U.S.C. § 307(d). The statute mandates the issuance of licenses if the 'public convenience, interest, or necessity will be served thereby.' 47 U.S.C. § 307(a)." [120]

The Court in *Red Lion* then noted:

> It is argued that even if at one time the lack of available frequencies for all who wished to use them justified the Government's choice of those who would best serve the public interest . . . this condition no longer prevails so that continuing control is not justified. To this there are several answers. Scarcity is not entirely a thing of the past. [121]

With the plethora of cable channels today, has spectrum scarcity now become a thing of the past? In *Turner Broadcasting System, Inc. v. FCC*, the Court held that the scarcity rationale does not apply to cable television:

> [C]able television does not suffer from the inherent limitations that characterize the broadcast medium . . . [S]oon there may be no practical limitation on the number of speakers who may use the cable medium. Nor is there any danger of physical interference between two cable speakers attempting to use the same channel. In light of these fundamental technological differences between broadcast and cable transmission, application of a more relaxed standard of scrutiny adopted in *Red Lion* and the other broadcast cases is inapt when determining the First Amendment validity of cable regulation." [122]

One might argue that, if the scarcity rationale does not apply to cable television, then it should not apply to broadcast television either, because a person who because of scarcity cannot start a broadcast channel can start a cable channel. [123] But the Court has not ruled on the question; in *Turner* it wrote: "Although courts and commentators have criticized the scarcity rationale since its inception, we have declined to question its continuing validity as support for our broadcast jurisprudence, and see no reason to do so here." [124]

In 1987, however, the FCC abolished the fairness doctrine, on First Amendment grounds, noting that technological developments and advancements in the telecommunications marketplace have provided a basis for the Supreme Court to reconsider its holding in *Red Lion*. The FCC's decision was upheld by the U.S.

Court of Appeals for the District of Columbia, and the Supreme Court declined to review the case. [125] The court of appeals did not rule on constitutional grounds, but rather concluded "that the FCC's decision that the fairness doctrine no longer served the public interest was neither arbitrary, capricious nor an abuse of discretion, and [we] are convinced that it would have acted on that finding to terminate the doctrine even in the absence of its belief that the doctrine was no longer constitutional." [126]

But, whether or not spectrum scarcity has become a thing of the past, it would apparently would not today justify governmental restrictions on "indecent" speech.

This is because, subsequent to the Court in *Turner* declining to question the applicability of the scarcity rationale to broadcast media, a plurality of justices noted, in *Denver Area Educational Telecommunications Consortium, Inc. v. FCC*, that, though spectrum scarcity continued to justify the "structural regulations at issue there [in *Turner*] (the 'must carry' rules), it has little to do with a case that involves the effects of television viewing on children. Those effects are the result of how parents and children view television programming, and how pervasive and intrusive that programming is. In that respect, cable and broadcast television differ little, if at all." [127] The plurality therefore upheld a federal statute that permits cable operators to prohibit indecent material on leased access channels. Thus, it appears that the Court today would not cite spectrum scarcity to justify restrictions on "indecent" material on broadcast media, but it might cite broadcast media's pervasiveness and intrusiveness.

Subsequent to *Denver Area*, in *United States v. Playboy Entertainment Group, Inc.*, the Court held that cable television has full First Amendment protection; i.e., content-based restrictions on cable television receive strict scrutiny. [128] Thus, if, as the Court said in *Denver Area*, cable and broadcast media differ little, if at all, with respect to the regulation of "indecent" material, and, if, as the Court said in *Playboy*, cable television receives strict scrutiny, then, arguably, broadcast media would also receive strict scrutiny with regard to restrictions on "indecent" material. [129] It is possible, however, that, if cable and broadcast media differ little, then the Court might apply *Pacifica* to both broadcast and cable, rather than to neither. In any event, as noted above, even if the Court were to continue to apply *Pacifica* to restrictions on broadcast media, this does not necessarily mean that it would uphold a ban on the broadcast of "indecent" language regardless of context, as *Pacifica* did not hold that an occasional expletive would justify a sanction.

Strict Scrutiny

We now consider the analysis that the Court might apply if it chooses not to apply *Pacifica* in deciding the constitutionality of a ban on the broadcast of "indecent" language regardless of context. The Court in *Pacifica*, as noted, offered two reasons why the FCC could prohibit offensive speech on broadcast media: "First, the broadcast media have established a uniquely pervasive presence in the lives of all Americans. Patently offensive, indecent material presented over the airwaves confronts the citizen, not only in public, but in the privacy of the home. . . .

Second, broadcasting is uniquely accessible to children, even those too young to read," and the government has an interest in the "well-being of its youth" and "in supporting 'parents' claim to authority in their own household.'" The first of these reasons apparently refers to adults as well as to children.

Ordinarily, when the government restricts speech, including "indecent" speech, on the basis of its content, the restriction, if challenged, will be found constitutional only if it satisfies "strict scrutiny." [130] This means that the government must prove that the restriction serves "to promote a compelling interest" and is "the least restrictive means to further the articulated interest." [131] The Court in *Pacifica* did not apply this test or any weaker First Amendment test, and did not explain why it did not. Its reason presumably was that the FCC's action restricted speech only on broadcast media. If, however, the Court were not to apply *Pacifica* in determining the constitutionality of a ban, during certain hours, on the broadcast of "indecent" language regardless of context, then it would apparently apply strict scrutiny.

If the Court were to apply strict scrutiny in making this determination, it seems unlikely that it would find the first reason cited in *Pacifica* — sparing citizens, including adults, from patently offensive or indecent words — to constitute a compelling governmental interest. The Court has held that the government may not prohibit the use of offensive words unless they "fall within [a] relatively few categories of instances," such as obscenity, fighting words, or words "thrust upon unwilling or unsuspecting viewers." [132]

If the Court were to apply strict scrutiny in determining the constitutionality of a ban, during certain hours, on the broadcast of "indecent" language regardless of context, it also might not find the second reason cited in *Pacifica* — protecting minors from patently offensive and indecent words and "supporting 'parents' claim to authority in their own household'" — to constitute a compelling governmental interest. When the Court considers the constitutionality of a restriction on speech, it ordinarily — even when the speech lacks full First Amendment protection and the court applies less than strict scrutiny — requires the government to "demonstrate that the recited harms are real, not merely conjectural, and that the regulation will in fact alleviate these harms in a direct and material way." [133] With respect to restrictions designed to deny minors access to sexually explicit material, by contrast, the courts appear to assume, without requiring evidence, that such material is harmful to minors, or to consider it "obscene as to minors," even if it is not obscene as to adults, and therefore not entitled to First Amendment protection with respect to minors, whether it is harmful to them or not. [134] A word used as a mere adjective or expletive, however, arguably does not constitute sexually oriented material. [135] Therefore, if a court applied strict scrutiny to decide the constitutionality of a ban, during certain hours, on the broadcast of "indecent" words regardless of context, then, in determining the presence of a compelling interest, the court might require the government to "demonstrate that the recited harms are real, not merely conjectural, and that the regulation will in fact alleviate these harms in a direct and material way." This could raise the question, not raised in *Pacifica*, of whether hearing such words is harmful to minors. More precisely, it might raise the question of whether hearing such words on broadcast radio and television is harmful to minors, even in light of the opportunities for minors to hear such words elsewhere. If the government failed to prove that hearing certain words on broadcast radio or television is harmful to minors, then a court would not find a compelling interest in censoring those words and might strike down the law.

It might still uphold the law, however, if it found that the law served the government's interest "in supporting 'parents' claim to authority in their own household,'" and that this is a compelling interest independent from the interest in protecting the well-being of minors. In *Ginsberg v. New York*, the Court referred to the state's interest in the well-being of its youth as "independent" from its interest in supporting "parents' claim to authority in their own household to direct the rearing of their children." [136] The holding in *Ginsberg*, however, did not turn on whether these interests are independent, and one might argue that they are not, because the government's interest in supporting parents lies in assisting them in protecting their children from harmful influences. If "indecent" words are not a harmful influence, then, arguably, the government has no interest, sufficient to override the First Amendment, in supporting parents in their efforts to prevent their children's access to them. It has also been argued that "a law that effectively *bans* all indecent programming . . . does not facilitate parental supervision. In my view, my right as a parent has been preempted, not facilitated, if I am told that certain programming will be banned from my . . . television. Congress cannot take away my right to decide what my children watch, absent some showing that my children are in fact at risk of harm from exposure to indecent programming." [137]

If the government could persuade a court that a ban, during certain hours, on the broadcast of "indecent" words regardless of context serves a compelling interest — either in protecting the well-being of minors or in supporting parents' claim to authority — the government would then have to prove that the ban was the least restrictive means to advance that interest. This might raise questions such as whether it is necessary to prohibit particular words on weekdays during school hours, solely to protect pre-school children and children who are home sick some days. In response to this question, the government could note that the broadcast in *Pacifica* was at 2 p.m. on a Tuesday, but was nevertheless considered a "time[] of the day when there is a reasonable risk that children may be in the audience." [138] More significantly, however, a court might find a ban too restrictive because it would prohibit the broadcast, between certain hours, of material, including works of art and other material with serious value, that would not attract substantial numbers of youthful viewers or listeners.

In conclusion, it appears that, if a court were to apply strict scrutiny to determine the constitutionality of a ban on the broadcast of "indecent" language regardless of context, then it might require the government to "demonstrate that the recited harms are real, not merely conjectural, and that the regulation will in fact alleviate these harms in a direct and material way." This would mean that the government would have to demonstrate a compelling governmental interest, such as that hearing "indecent" words on broadcast radio and television is harmful to minors, despite the likelihood that minors hear such words elsewhere, or that banning "indecent" words is necessary to support parents' authority in their own household. If the government could not demonstrate a compelling governmental interest, then the court might find the ban unconstitutional. Even if the government could demonstrate a compelling interest, a court might find the ban unconstitutional if it applied to material with serious value, at least if such material would not attract substantial numbers of youthful viewers or listeners.

Whether a court would apply strict scrutiny would depend upon whether, in light of the proliferation of cable television, it finds *Pacifica* to remain applicable to broadcast media. If a court does find that *Pacifica* remains applicable to broadcast media, then the court would be faced with questions that *Pacifica* did not decide: whether, on broadcast radio and television during hours when children are likely to be in the audience, the government may prohibit an "indecent" word used as an occasional expletive, or in material that would not attract substantial numbers of youthful viewers or listeners.

ENDNOTES

[1] The FCC's indecency regulations only apply to broadcast radio and television, and not to cable television. The distinction between broadcast and cable television arises in part from the fact that the rationale for regulation of broadcast media — the dual problems of spectrum scarcity and signal interference — do not apply in the context of cable. As a result, regulation of cable television is entitled to heightened First Amendment scrutiny. *See Turner Broadcasting v. Federal Communications Commission*, 512 U.S. 622 (1994). Cable television is also distinguished from broadcast television by the fact that cable involves a voluntary act whereby a subscriber affirmatively chooses to bring the material into his or home. *See Cruz v. Ferre*, 755 F.2d 1415 (11th Cir. 1985).

[2] The final section of this report ("Would prohibiting the broadcast of 'indecent' words regardless of context violate the First Amendment?") was written by Henry Cohen; the rest of the report was written by Angie A. Welborn.

[3] See *In the Matter of Complaints Against Various Broadcast Licensees Regarding Their Airing of the "Golden Globe Awards" Program*, 18 F.C.C. Rcd. 19859 (2003).
[4] *Id.* at 2.
[5] *Id.*
[6] *Id.* at 3.
[7] *Id.*
[8] *FCC Chairman Seeks Reversal on Profanity*, Washington Post, January 14, 2004, at E01.
[9] *In the Matter of Complaints Against Various Broadcast Licensees Regarding Their Airing of the "Golden Globe Awards" Program*, File No. EB-03-IH-0110 (March 18, 2004).
[10] [http://hraunfoss.fcc.gov/edocs_public/attachmatch/DOC-243435A1.pdf].
[11] *Complaints Against Various Television Licensees Concerning Their February 1, 2004, Broadcast of the Super Bowl XXXVIII Halftime Show*, File No. EB-04-IH-0011 (September 22, 2004).
[12] *Id.*
[13] 18 U.S.C. § 1464. "Radio communication" includes broadcast television, as the term is defined as "the transmission by radio of writing, signs, signals, pictures, and sounds of all kinds." 47 U.S.C. § 153(33).
[14] 47 U.S.C. § 503(b).
[15] 438 U.S. 726 (1978).
[16] The United State Court of Appeals for the District of Columbia Circuit had reversed the Commission's order. *See* 556 F.2d 9 (D.C. Cir. 1977). The Commission appealed that decision to the Supreme Court. The Court granted certiorari and reversed the lower court's opinion.
[17] 438 U.S. at 732.
[18] *Id.*
[19] *Id.* at 742.
[20] *Id.* at 731; see, *In the Matter of a Citizen's Complaint Against Pacifica Foundation Station WBAI (FM), New York, New York*, 56 F.C.C.2d 94 (1975).
[21] *In the Matter of Pacifica Foundation, Inc. d/b/a Pacifica Radio Los Angeles, California*, 2 F.C.C. Rcd. 2698 (1987). Two other orders handed down the same day articulate the Commission's clarified indecency standard. *See also In the Matter of the Regents of the University of California*, 2 F.C.C. Rcd. 2703 (1987); *In the Matter of*

Infinity Broadcasting Corporation of Pennsylvania, 2 F.C.C. Rcd. 2705 (1987).

[22] The Commission noted Arbitron ratings indicating that a number of children remain in the local audience well after 10 p.m. *See* 2 F.C.C. Rcd. 1698, ¶ 16.

[23] 2 F.C.C. Rcd. 2698, ¶¶ 12 and 15.

[24] 852 F.2d 1332, 1344 (1988).

[25] Pub. L. 100-459, § 608.

[26] *Enforcement of Prohibitions Against Broadcast Obscenity and Indecency*, 4 F.C.C. Rcd. 457 (1988).

[27] *Action for Children's Television v. Federal Communications Commission (ACT II)*, 932 F.2d 1504 (1991), *cert. denied*, 503 U.S. 913 (1992).

[28] *Id.* at 1509.

[29] Pub. L. 102-356, § 16, 47 U.S.C. § 303 note.

[30] *In the Matter of Enforcement of Prohibitions Against Broadcast Indecency in 18 U.S.C. 1464*, 8 F.C.C. Rcd. 704 (1993).

[31] *Action for Children's Television v. Federal Communications Commission*, 11 F.3d 170 (D.C. Cir. 1993).

[32] 8 F.C.C. Rcd. at 705 - 706.

[33] 11 F.3d at 171.

[34] *Id.*

[35] *Action for Children's Television v. Federal Communications Commission*, 15 F.3d 186 (D.C. Cir. 1994).

[36] *Action for Children's Television v. Federal Communications Commission (ACT III)*, 58 F.3d 654 (D.C. Cir. 1995), *cert. denied*, 516 U.S. 1043 (1996).

[37] 58 F.3d at 656.

[38] *Enforcement of Prohibitions Against Broadcast Indecency in 18 U.S.C. § 1464*, 10 F.C.C. Rcd. 10558 (1995); 47 C.F.R. 73.3999(b). Subsection (b) prohibits the broadcast of material which is obscene without any reference to time of day. Broadcast obscenity will not be discussed in this report. For more information on obscenity, see CRS Report 95-804, *Obscenity and Indecency: Constitutional Principles and Federal Statutes*, and CRS Report 98-670, *Obscenity, Child Pornography, and Indecency: Recent Developments and Pending Issues*.

[39] 60 FR 44439 (August 28, 1995).

[40] Enforcement actions based on televised broadcast indecency are rare. However, the Commission recently issued a *Notice of Apparent*

Liability for the broadcast of indecent material during a televised morning news program. During the program, the show's hosts interviewed performers with a production entitled "Puppetry of the Penis," who appeared wearing capes but were otherwise nude. A performer's penis was exposed during the broadcast. *See In the Matter of Young Broadcasting of San Francisco, Inc.*, File No. EB-02-IH-0786 (January 27, 2004). *See also In the Matter of Complaints Against Various Licensees Regarding Their Broadcast of the Fox Television Network Program "Married by America" on April 7, 2003*, File No. EB-03-IH-0162 (October 12, 2004).

[41] According to statute, the maximum fine per violation is $25,000. *See* 47 U.S.C. 503(b)(2)(A). However, the maximum forfeiture amount was increased to $32,500 pursuant to the Debt Collection Improvement Act of 1996, Public Law 104-134, which amends the Federal Civil Monetary Penalty Inflation Adjustment Act of 1990, Public Law 101-410. *See* 47 C.F.R. 1.80.

[42] *See* fn 93, *infra* and accompanying text. Regulations set a maximum forfeiture of $325,000 for any single act or failure to act, which arguably limits the forfeiture for a single broadcast. *See* 47 C.F.R. 1.80.

[43] *See In the Matter of Industry Guidance on the Commission's Case Law Interpreting 18 U.S.C. § 1464 and Enforcement Policies Regarding Broadcast Indecency*, File No. EB-00-IH-0089 (April 6, 2001). [http://www.fcc.gov/eb/Orders/2001/fcc01090.html]

[44] The Commission's Enforcement Bureau initially dismissed the complaint against broadcast licensees for airing the 2003 Golden Globe Awards, in which performer Bono uttered the phrase "this is really, really f[***]ing brilliant," due primarily to the fact that the language in question did not describe or depict sexual and excretory activities or organs. 18 F.C.C. Rcd. 19859 (2003). The decision of the Enforcement Bureau has since been reversed. *See infra* regarding this case.

[45] *Id.*
[46] *Id.*
[47] *Id.* at 5.
[48] *Notice of Apparent Liability, State University of New York*, 8 F.C.C. Rcd. 456 (1993).
[49] *Id.*
[50] *See* note 35, *supra*.

[51] *Notice of Apparent Liability, KGB Incorporated*, 7 F.C.C. Rcd. 3207 (1992). *See also Great American Television and Radio Company, Inc.*, 6 F.C.C. Rcd. 3692 (1990); *WIOD, Inc.*, 6 F.C.C. Rcd. 3704 (1989).
[52] 6 F.C.C. Rcd. 3692.
[53] *See* note 35, *supra*.
[54] *Notice of Apparent Liability, Citicasters Co.*, 13 F.C.C. Rcd. 22004 (1998).
[55] The Commission has recently indicated that "the mere fact that specific words or phrases are not sustained or repeated does not mandate a finding that material that is otherwise patently offensive to the broadcast medium is not indecent." *In the Matter of Complaints Against Various Broadcast Licensees Regarding the Airing of the "Golden Globe Awards" Program*, File No. EB-03-IH-0110 (March 18, 2004). *See* section entitled Golden Globe Awards Decision *infra*.
[56] *L.M. Communications of South Carolina, Inc.*, 7 F.C.C. Rcd. 1595 (1992).
[57] *Id*.
[58] *See Notice of Apparent Liability, Temple Radio, Inc.*, 12 F.C.C. Rcd. 21828 (1997); *Notice of Apparent Liability, EZ New Orleans, Inc.*, 12 F.C.C. Rcd. 4147 (1997).
[59] *Notice of Apparent Liability, Rusk Corporation, Radio Station KLOL*, 5 F.C.C. Rcd. 6332 (1990).
[60] *In the Matter of Application for Review of the Dismissal of an Indecency Complaint Against King Broadcasting Co.*, 5 F.C.C. Rcd. 2971 (1990).
[61] *Id*.
[62] *Id*.
[63] The Commission declined to impose a forfeiture on the broadcast licensees named in the complaint because they were not "on notice" regarding the new interpretations of the Commission's regulations regarding broadcast indecency and the newly adopted definition of profanity. The Commission also indicated that it will not use its decision in this case adversely against the licensees during the license renewal process.
[64] *In the Matter of Complaints Against Various Broadcast Licensees Regarding Their Airing of the "Golden Globe Awards" Program*, File No. EB-03-IH-0110 at 4 (March 18, 2004).
[65] *Id*.
[66] *Id*. at 5.

[67] *Id.* at 6. *See* section entitled Dwelling or Repetition of Potentially Indecent Material *supra*.
[68] *Id.*
[69] *Id.* at 7. It should be noted that, although in this case the Commission found that the broadcast in question was both indecent and profane, there are certain to be words that could be deemed "profane," but do not fit the Commission's definition of "indecent." Under the newly adopted definition of "profanity," many words could arguably be found "profane" because they provoke "violent resentment" or are otherwise "grossly offensive," but not be found "indecent" because they do not refer to any sexual or excretory activity or organ or even "inherently" have a sexual connotation, as the Commission found the phrase that Bono uttered to have. Presumably, it is these words that the Commission will consider on a caseby- case basis.
[70] *Id.* at 7, citing Black's Law Dictionary 1210 (6thed. 1990) and American Heritage College Dictionary 1112 (4th ed. 2002).
[71] *Id.*, citing *Tallman v. United States*, 465 F.2d 282, 286 (7th Cir. 1972).
[72] *Id.*
[73] *Complaints Against Various Television Licensees Concerning Their February 1, 2004, Broadcast of the Super Bowl XXXVIII Halftime Show*, File No. EB-04-IH-0011 (September 22, 2004).
[74] *Id.* at ¶ 11.
[75] *Id.* at ¶ 13.
[76] *Id.* at ¶ 14.
[77] *Id.*
[78] *Id.* at ¶¶ 17 - 24.
[79] 47 C.F.R. 1.80(f)(3).
[80] 47 C.F.R. 1.80(f)(4).
[81] Procedures for appealing Commission orders are set forth in 47 U.S.C. 402.
[82] For a complete list of recent actions related to broadcast indecency, see [http://www.fcc.gov/eb/broadcast/obscind.html].
[83] *In the Matter of Infinity Broadcasting, et al.*, EB-02-IH-0685 (October 2, 2003).
[84] *Id.* at 8.
[85] *Id.* at 9. The Commission noted that the contest portion of the broadcast in question lasted over an hour and was reproduced in a 203-page transcript.

[86] *See In the Matter of Viacom Inc., Infinity Radio Inc., et. al.*, FCC 04-268 (November 23, 2004). [http://hraunfoss.fcc.gov/edocs_public/attachmatch/FCC-04-268A1.pdf]. The decree also covers several other actions pending against Viacom-owned Infinity Radio stations and broadcast television stations, but does not cover the proceedings related to the Super Bowl halftime show discussed *supra*.

[87] *In the Matter of Clear Channel Broadcasting Licenses, Inc., et al.*, File No. EB-02-IH- 0261 (January 27, 2004).

[88] *Id.* at 4.

[89] *Id.* at 5.

[90] *Id.* at 6.

[91] *Id.*

[92] *In the Matter of Clear Channel Broadcasting Licensees*, File No. EB-03-IH — 159 (April 8, 2004).

[93] *See* Statement of Commissioner Michael J. Copps, [http://hraunfoss.fcc.gov/edocs_public/attachmatch/DOC-245911A1.pdf], p. 2.

[94] *See In the Matter of Clear Channel Communications, Inc.*, FCC 04-128 (June 9, 2004) at [http://hraunfoss.fcc.gov/edocs_public/attachmatch/FCC-04-128A1.pdf].

[95] *Id.* at 7.

[96] H.R. 3687. The FCC's indecency regulation prescribes the 10 p.m.-to-6 a.m. "safe harbor" for "indecent programming." No comparable regulation addresses profane programming. One might argue, therefore, that the ban on profane programming under 18 U.S.C. § 1464, as it exists now and as it would be amended by H.R. 3687, would apply around the clock. This reading of the statute, however, might render it unconstitutional (*see* note 27, *supra*), and a court might reject it for that reason. *See*, United States v. X-Citement Video, Inc., 513 U.S. 64, 69 (1994) ("a statute is to be construed where fairly possible so as to avoid substantial constitutional questions").

[97] H.Rept. 108-434.

[98] Roll Call No. 55, 150 Cong. Rec. H1035 (daily ed. March 11, 2004).

[99] S.Rept. 108-253.

[100] The Senate committee also added a new title to the original bill, entitled the "Children's Protection from Violent Programming Act."

[101] S.Amdt. 3235, as amended.

[102] *See* conference report for H.R. 4200, H.Rept. 108-767.

[103] This bill appears to be substantially similar to H.R. 3717, as reported by the House Committee on Energy and Commerce, on March 3, 2004.
[104] H.Amdt. 10. The FCC's policy statement on broadcast indecency was released on April 6, 2001, and can be found here [http://www.fcc.gov/eb/Orders/2001/fcc01090.html].
[105] 438 U.S. 726 (1978). The FCC's action was to issue "a declaratory order granting the complaint," and "state that the order would be 'associated with the station's license file,'" which means that the FCC could consider it when it came time for the station's license renewal. *Id.* at 730.
[106] 521 U.S. 844, 868 (1997) (noting that "the history of the extensive regulation of the broadcast medium" and "the scarcity of available frequencies" are factors "not present in cyberspace," and striking down parts of the Communications Decency Act of 1996). The Court also cited *Pacifica* with approval in *United States v. Playboy Entertainment Group, Inc.*, 529 U.S. 803, 813-814 (1998), and in *Ashcroft v. Free Speech Coalition*, 535 U.S. 234, 245 (2002).
[107] *Pacifica, supra*, 438 U.S. at 750. A federal court of appeals subsequently held unconstitutional a federal statute that banned "indecent" broadcasts 24 hours a day, but, in a later case, the same court upheld the present statute, 47 U.S.C. § 303 note, which bans "indecent" broadcasts from 6 a.m. to 10 p.m. Action for Children's Television v. FCC, 932 F.2d 1504 (D.C. Cir. 1991), *cert. denied*, 503 U.S. 913 (1992); Action for Children's Television v. FCC, 58 F.3d 654 (D.C. Cir. 1995) (en banc), *cert. denied*, 516 U.S. 1043 (1996).
[108] *Id.* at 750, n.29.
[109] *Id.* at 746 n.22. These two sentences and the text accompanying the next footnote, although part of Justice Stevens' opinion, are in a part of the opinion (IV-B) joined by only two other justices. Every other quotation from *Pacifica* in this report was from a part of the opinion that a majority of the justices joined.
[110] *Id.* at 746.
[111] There also appears to be some tension between, on the one hand, Justice Stevens' distinction in *Pacifica* between a point of view and the way in which it is expressed, and, on the other hand, the Court's statement in *Cohen v. California* "that much linguistic expression serves a dual communicative function: it conveys not only ideas capable of relatively precise, detached explication, but otherwise inexpressible emotions as well. In fact, words are often chosen as

much for their emotive as their cognitive force. We cannot sanction the view that the Constitution, while solicitous of the cognitive content of individual speech, has little or no regard for that emotive function which, practically speaking, may often be the more important element of the overall message sought to be communicated." 403 U.S. 15, 26 (1971) (upholding the First Amendment right, in the corridor of a courthouse, to wear a jacket bearing the words "F[***] the Draft"). Arguably, Carlin's use of "indecent" words not only served an emotive purpose, but served to indicate the precise words to whose censorship he was objecting. Yet *Pacifica* was decided after *Cohen*, which suggests that *Cohen* does not lessen the precedential value of *Pacifica*.

[112] Miller v. California, 413 U.S. 15, 27, 24 (1973). In addition, in striking down parts of the Communications Decency Act of 1996, the Court expressed concern that the statute may "extend to discussions about prison rape or safe sexual practices, artistic images that include nude subjects, and arguably the card catalogue of the Carnegie Library." *Reno v. ACLU, supra*, 521 U.S. at 878. And, in striking down a federal statute that prohibited child pornography that was produced without the use of an actual child, the Court expressed concern that the statute "prohibits speech despite its serious literary, artistic, political, or scientific value." Ashcroft v. Free Speech Coalition, 535 U.S. 234, 246 (2002). In neither of these cases, however, did the Court state that its holding turned on the statute's application to works of serious value.

[113] 390 U.S. 629 (1968).

[114] *Pacifica, supra*, 438 U.S. at 731-732.

[115] *Id.* at 732 (distinguishing "indecent" from "obscene" and "profane" in 18 U.S.C. § 1464).

[116] *Id.* at 740.

[117] *Id.* at 748-750.

[118] 395 U.S. 367, 369 (1969).

[119] *Id.* at 388.

[120] *Id.* at 394.

[121] *Id.* at 396.

[122] 512 U.S. 622, 639 (1994). In *Turner*, the Court held that the "must carry" rules, which "require cable television systems to devote a portion of their channels to the transmission of local broadcast television stations," *id.* at 626, were content-neutral and therefore not

subject to strict scrutiny. The Court remanded and ultimately upheld the rules. Turner Broadcasting System, Inc., 520 U.S. 180 (1997).

[123] In the court of appeals decision upholding the current statute that bans "indecent" broadcasts from 6 a.m. to 10 p.m., a dissenting judge wrote of "the utterly irrational distinction that Congress has created between *broadcast* and *cable* operators. No one disputes that cable exhibits more and worse indecency than does broadcast. And cable television is certainly pervasive in our country." Action for Children's Television v. FCC, *supra*, 58 F.3d at 671 (emphasis in original) (Edwards, C.J., dissenting).

[124] 512 U.S. at 638 (citation omitted).

[125] Syracuse Peace Council v. FCC, 867 F.2d 654 (D.C. Cir. 1989), *cert. denied*, 493 U.S. 1019 (1990).

[126] *Id.* at 669. In *Arkansas AFL-CIO v. FCC*, 11 F.3d 1430 (8th Cir. 1993) (en banc), the court of appeals held that Congress had not codified the fairness doctrine and that the FCC's decision to eliminate it was a reasonable interpretation of the statutory requirement that licensees operate in the public interest.

[127] 518 U.S. 727, 748 (1996). The plurality added that cable television "is as 'accessible to children' as over-the-air broadcasting, if not more so," has also "established a uniquely pervasive presence in the lives of all Americans," and can also "'confron[t] the citizen' in 'the privacy of the home,' . . . with little or no prior warning." *Id.* at 744-745. Justice Souter concurred that "today's plurality opinion rightly observes that the characteristics of broadcast radio that rendered indecency particularly threatening in *Pacifica*, that is, its intrusion into the house and accessibility to children, are also present in the case of cable television. ...." *Id.* at 776.

[128] 529 U.S. 803, 813 (2000) (striking down a federal statute that required distributors to fully scramble or fully block signal bleed to non-subscribers to cable channels; "signal bleed" refers to the audio or visual portions of cable television programs that non- subscribers to a cable channel may be able to hear or see despite the fact that the programs have been scrambled to prevent the non-subscribers from hearing or seeing them).

[129] An earlier district court case held that *Pacifica* does not apply to cable television because of several differences between cable and broadcasting. For one, "[i]n the cable medium, the physical scarcity that justifies content regulation in broadcasting is not present." For another, as a subscriber medium, "cable TV is not an intruder but an

invitee whose invitation can be carefully circumscribed." Community Television v. Wilkinson, 611 F. Supp. 1099 (D. Utah 1985), *aff'd*, 800 F.2d 989 (10th Cir. 1986), *aff'd*, 480 U.S. 926 (1987) (striking down Utah Cable Television Programming Decency Act). The court of appeals did not discuss the constitutional issue beyond stating that it agreed with the district court's reasons for its holding. 800 F.2d at 991. A summary affirmance by the Supreme Court, as in this case, is "an affirmance of the judgment only," and does not indicate approval of the reasoning of the court below. Mandel v. Bradley, 432 U.S. 173, 176 (1977).

[130] Sable Communications of California v. Federal Communications Commission, 492 U.S. 115 (1989); Action for Children's Television v. FCC, *supra*, 932 F.2d at 1509.

[131] *Id.* at 126.

[132] Cohen v. California, *supra*, 403 U.S. at 19, 21. Under *Pacifica*, broadcast media do thrust words upon unwilling or unsuspecting viewers, but, if a court were to apply strict scrutiny to a ban on the broadcast of "indecent" language regardless of context, then it would not be following *Pacifica*.

[133] *Turner Broadcasting*, *supra*, 512 U.S. at 664 (incidental restriction on speech). *See also*, Edenfield v. Fane, 507 U.S. 761, 770-771 (1993) (restriction on commercial speech); Nixon v. Shrink Missouri Government PAC, 528 U.S. 377, 392 (2000) (restriction on campaign contributions). In all three of these cases, the government had restricted less-than-fully protected speech, so the Court did not apply strict scrutiny. Because offensive words are apparently entitled to full First Amendment protection (except under *Pacifica* and in the instances cited in *Cohen v. California*, quoted in the text above), it seems all the more likely that the Court, if it applied strict scrutiny instead of *Pacifica* to a challenge to a ban on the broadcast of "indecent" words regardless of context, would require the government to demonstrate that harms it recites are real and that the ban would alleviate these harms in a direct and material way.

[134] Interactive Digital Software Association v. St. Louis County, Missouri, 329 F.3d 954, 959 (8th Cir. 2003). The Supreme Court has "recognized that there is a compelling interest in protecting the physical and psychological well-being of minors. This interest extends to shielding minors from the influence of literature that is not obscene by adult standards." *Sable*, *supra*, 492 U.S. at 126. The Court has also upheld a state law banning the distribution to minors of "so-called

'girlie' magazines" even as it acknowledged that "[i]t is very doubtful that this finding [that such magazines are "a basic factor in impairing the ethical and moral development of our youth"] expresses an accepted scientific fact." Ginsberg v. New York, *supra*, 390 U.S. at 631, 641. "To sustain state power to exclude [such material from minors]," the Court wrote, "requires only that we be able to say that it was not irrational for the legislature to find that exposure to material condemned by the statute is harmful to minors." *Id.* at 641. *Ginsberg* thus "invokes the much less exacting 'rational basis' standard of review," rather than strict scrutiny. *Interactive Digital Software Association, supra*, 329 F.3d at 959.

A federal district court wrote:

We are troubled by the absence of evidence of harm presented both before Congress and before us that the viewing of signal bleed of sexually explicit programming causes harm to children and that the avoidance of this harm can be recognized as a compelling State interest. We recognize that the Supreme Court's jurisprudence does not require empirical evidence. Only some minimal amount of evidence is required when sexually explicit programming and children are involved.

Playboy Entertainment Group, Inc. v. United States, 30 F. Supp.2d 702, 716 (D. Del. 1998), *aff'd*, 529 U.S. 803 (2000). The district court therefore found that the statute served a compelling governmental interest, though it held it unconstitutional because it found that the statute did not constitute the least restrictive means to advance the interest. The Supreme Court affirmed on the same ground, apparently assuming the existence of a compelling governmental interest, but finding a less restrictive means that could have been used.

In another case, a federal court of appeals, upholding the current statute that bans "indecent" broadcasts from 6 a.m. to 10 p.m., noted "that the Supreme Court has recognized that the Government's interest in protecting children extends beyond shielding them from physical and psychological harm. The statute that the Court found constitutional in *Ginsberg* sought to protect children from exposure to materials that would 'impair [their] *ethical and moral* development. . . . Congress does not need the testimony of psychiatrists and social scientists in order to take note of the coarsening of impressionable minds that can result from a persistent exposure to sexually explicit material. . . ." Action for Children's Television v. FCC, *supra*, 58 F.3d at 662 (brackets and italics supplied by the court). A dissenting judge in the case noted that, "[t]here is not one iota of evidence in the record . . . to support the claim that exposure to indecency is harmful — indeed, the nature of the alleged 'harm' is never explained." *Id.* at 671 (D.C. Cir. 1995) (Edwards, C.J., dissenting).

[135] The full Commission's decision in the Bono case stated that "any use of that word or a variation, in any context, inherently has a sexual connotation." But this does not necessarily mean that it is sexually oriented enough to cause the courts to assume without evidence that it is harmful to minors.

[136] *Ginsberg, supra,* 390 at 640, 639. *See also,* Action for Children's Television v. FCC, *supra,* 58 F.3d at 661.

[137] Action for Children's Television v. FCC, *supra,* 58 F.3d at 670 (emphasis in original) (Edwards, C.J., dissenting).

[138] *Pacifica, supra,* 438 U.S. at 732.

Chapter 2

V-CHIP AND TV RATINGS: MONITORING CHILDREN'S ACCESS TO TV PROGRAMMING[*]

Patricia Moloney Figliola

PREFACE

To assist parents in supervising the television viewing habits of their children, the Communications Act of 1934 (as amended by the Telecommunications Act of 1996) requires that, as of January 1, 2000, new television sets with screens 13 inches or larger sold in the United States be equipped with a "V-chip" to control access to programming that parents find objectionable. Use of the V-chip is optional. In March 1998, the Federal Communications Commission (FCC) adopted the industry developed ratings system to be used in conjunction with the V-chip. Congress and the FCC have continued monitoring implementation of the V-chip. Some are concerned that it is not effective in curbing the amount of TV violence viewed by children and want further legislation.

Both the Senate and the House of Representatives held hearings and introduced bills on broadcast indecency and violence. S. 161 and H.R. 3914, companion bills both named the Children's Protection from Violent Programming Act, would have required the FCC to investigate and report to Congress on the effectiveness of the Vchip.

---

[*] Excerpted from CRS Report RL32729 dated January 10, 2005

No further action was taken on these bills. S. 2056, the Broadcast Decency Enforcement Act, was originally aimed only at increasing the penalties for broadcasters transmitting obscene, indecent, and profane language, but was amended to include language substantially similar to S. 161. S. 2056 was later added as an amendment to S. 2400, the Ronald Reagan National Defense Authorization Act for FY2005; the language was later removed in conference and was not included in the final version of the bill that was signed into law (H.R. 4200).

The FCC is conducting an ongoing inquiry regarding the "presentation of violent programming and its impact on children (FCC 04-175)." Comments and replies were due in this proceeding on October 15 and November 15, 2004, respectively. There is no set timetable for further action.

Congress may wish to consider a number of possible options to support parents in controlling their children's access to certain programming. Some of these options would require only further educational outreach to parents, while others would require at least regulatory, if not legislative, action. Specifically, Congress may wish to consider ways to promote awareness of the V-chip and the ratings system; whether the current set of media-specific ratings will remain viable in the future or whether a uniform system would better serve the needs of consumers; and whether independent ratings systems and an "open" V-chip that would allow consumers to select the ratings systems they use would be more appropriate than the current system.

BACKGROUND

Recent research indicates that 89% of parents are "somewhat" to "very" concerned that "their children are being exposed to too much inappropriate content in entertainment media." [1] Further, parents cited television as the medium that caused them the most concern. [2] Although exposure to inappropriate material has long been a concern to parents, only since the Telecommunications Act of 1996 [3] has there been a nationwide effort to provide parents with a tool to control their children's television viewing — the V-chip. [4]

The V-chip, which reads an electronic code transmitted with the television signal (cable or broadcast), [5] is used in conjunction with a television programming rating system. Using a remote control, parents can

---

* Excerpted from CRS Report RL32729 dated January 10, 2005

enter a password and then program into the television set which ratings are acceptable and which are unacceptable. The chip automatically blocks the display of any programs deemed unacceptable; use of the V-chip by parents is entirely optional. [6]

As of January 1, 2000, all new television sets with a picture screen 13 inches or greater sold in the United States must be equipped with the V-chip. [7] Additionally, some companies also offer stand-alone devices that can work with non-V-chip TV sets.

DEVELOPMENT OF THE V-CHIP RATINGS SYSTEM

The initial ratings system was developed during 1996 and 1997, but encountered criticism from within Congress as well as from groups such as the National Parent-Teacher Association. In response to those concerns, an expanded ratings system was adopted on July 10, 1997, and went into effect October 1, 1997.

Initial Ratings System

The first step in implementing the mandate of the law was to create a ratings system for television programs, analogous to the one developed and adopted for movies by the Motion Picture Association of America (MPAA) in 1968. The law urged the television industry to develop a voluntary ratings system acceptable to the FCC, and the rules for transmitting the rating, within one year of enactment. The ratings system is intended to convey information regarding "sexual, violent or other indecent material about which parents should be informed before it is displayed to children, provided that nothing in [the law] should be construed to authorize any rating of video programming on the basis of its political or religious content." [8]

After initial opposition, media and entertainment industry executives met with then-President Clinton on February 29, 1996, and agreed to develop the ratings system because of political pressure to do so. Many in the television industry were opposed to the V-chip, fearing that it would reduce viewership and reduce advertising revenues. They also questioned whether it violated the First Amendment. Industry executives said they would not challenge the law immediately, but left the option open should they deem it necessary.

Beginning in March 1996, a group of television industry executives [9] under the leadership of Jack Valenti, then-President of the MPAA (and a leader in creating the movie ratings), met to develop a TV ratings system. On December 19, 1996, the group proposed six age-based ratings (TV-Y, TV-Y7, TV-G, TV-PG, TV-14 and TVM), including text explanations of what each represented in terms of program content. In January 1997, the ratings began appearing in the upper left-hand corner of TV screens for 15 seconds at the beginning of programs, and were published in some television guides. Thus, the ratings system was used even before V-chips were installed in new TV sets.

Ratings are assigned to shows by the TV Parental Guidelines Monitoring Board. The board has a chairman and six members each from the broadcast television industry, the cable industry, and the program production community. The chairman also selects five non-industry members from the advocacy community, for a total of 24 members.

News shows and sports programming are not rated. Local broadcast affiliates may override the rating given a particular show and assign it another rating.

The Current "S-V-L-D" Ratings System

Critics of the initial ratings system argued that the ratings provided no information on why a particular program received a certain rating. Some advocated an "S-V-L" system (sex, violence, language) to indicate with letters why a program received a particular rating, possibly with a numeric indicator or jointly with an age-based rating. Another alternative was the Home Box Office/Showtime system of ten ratings such as MV (mild violence), V (violence), and GV (graphic violence).

In response to the criticism, most of the television industry agreed to a revised ratings system (see box, below) on July 10, 1997, that went into effect October 1, 1997. The revised ratings system added designators to indicate whether a program received a particular rating because of sex (S), violence (V), language (L), or suggestive dialogue (D). A designator for fantasy violence (FV) was added for children's programming in the TV-Y7 category. On March 12, 1998, the FCC approved the revised ratings system, along with V-chip technical standards, and the effective date for installing them. [10]

In May 1999, the FCC created a V-chip Task Force, chaired by then-Commissioner Gloria Tristani. Among other things, the task force was charged with ensuring that the blocking technology was available and that ratings were being transmitted ("encoded") with TV programs; educating parents about V-chip; and gathering information on the availability, usage, and effectiveness of the V-chip. The task force issued several reports and surveys [http://www.fcc.gov/vchip]. A February 2000 task force survey found that most broadcast, cable, and premium cable networks, and syndicators, were transmitting ratings ("encoding") and those that were not either planned to do so in the near future or were exempt sports or news networks. Of the major broadcast and cable networks, only NBC and Black Entertainment Television do not use the S-V-L-D indicators, using the original ratings system instead.

	U.S. Television Industry's Revised TV Ratings System
TV Y	**TV-Y All Children** This program is designed to be appropriate for all children. Whether animated or live-action, the themes and elements in this program are specifically designed for a very young audience, including children from ages 2-6. This program is not expected to frighten younger children.
TV Y7	**TV-Y7 Directed to Older Children** This program is designed for children age 7 and above. It may be more appropriate for children who have acquired the developmental skills needed to distinguish between make-believe and reality. Themes and elements in this program may include mild fantasy or comedic violence, or may frighten children under the age of 7. Therefore, parents may wish to consider the suitability of this program for their very young children.
TV Y7 FV	**TV-Y7-FV Directed to Older Children-Fantasy Violence** For those programs where fantasy violence may be more intense or more combative than other programs in the TV-Y7 category, such programs will be designated TV-Y7-FV.
TV G	**TV-G General Audience** Most parents would find this program appropriate for all ages. Although this rating does not signify a program designed specifically for children, most parents may let younger children watch this program unattended. It contains little or no violence, no strong language and little or no sexual dialogue or situations.
TV PG	**TV-PG Parental Guidance Suggested** This program contains material that parents may find unsuitable for younger children. Many parents may want to watch it with their younger children. The theme itself may call for parental guidance and/or the program contains one or more of the following: moderate violence (V), some sexual situations (S), infrequent coarse language (L), or some suggestive dialogue (D).
TV 14	**TV-14 Parents Strongly Cautioned** This program contains some material that many parents would find unsuitable for children under 14 years of age. Parents are strongly urged to exercise greater care in monitoring this program and are cautioned against letting children under the age of 14 watch unattended. This program contains one or more of the following: intense violence (V), intense sexual situations (S), strong coarse language (L), or intensely suggestive dialogue (D).
TV MA	**TV-MA Mature Audience Only** This program is specifically designed to be viewed by adults and therefore may be unsuitable for children under 17. This program contains one or more of the following: graphic violence (V), explicit sexual activity (S), or crude indecent language (L).

CONGRESSIONAL ACTION: 108TH CONGRESS

During 2003 and 2004, the television industry and the FCC faced increasing scrutiny for what was perceived by many in Congress, as well as the public, as a sharp increase in the amount of indecent programming. The two most notable events that took place with respect to this issue were the FCC's determination that the use of the "f-word" by an artist during an award ceremony was not indecent and, four days later, an incident during the Super Bowl XXXVIII half-time show that included a performance in which one of the entertainer's breasts was revealed. Both the Senate and House of Representatives held hearings, considered legislation, and passed resolutions [11] related to broadcast indecency and violence. [12]

Senate

The Committee on Commerce, Science, and Transportation and its Subcommittee on Science, Technology, and Space each held one hearing during the 108th Congress related to broadcast indecency and the V-chip; two bills specific to the V-chip and the ratings system were considered. [13]

Hearings

At the February 11, 2004, hearing, held by the full committee, the members heard testimony from the five FCC commissioners on how best to protect children from violent and indecent programming and the adequacy of current regulations protecting children from such broadcasts. The hearing had been scheduled prior to the Super Bowl XXXVIII event, discussed earlier, to focus on violence on television, but both committee members and the FCC commissioners focused much of the hearing on the Super Bowl event. Although the focus of most of the discussion was on the amount of indecency being broadcast and what could and should be done to curb it, there was some discussion, particularly by FCC Commissioner Kathleen Abernathy, about the V-chip and ratings system.

On September 28, 2004, the Subcommittee on Science, Technology, and Space held a hearing on whether the existing ratings systems for the video game, television, and motion picture industries were effective in assisting consumers in discerning what is appropriate entertainment for their children. Witnesses testified from the MPAA; [14] the Entertainment Software Rating Board (ESRB); [15] the Kids Risk Project at the Harvard School of Public

Health; [16] the Children and the Media Program of Children Now; [17] PSV Ratings; [18] and the TV Parental Guidelines Monitoring Board. [19] In general, the industry representatives who testified believe the current ratings systems employed by television, movies, and video games remain viable. The PSV representative cited the growing number of independent rating systems [20] as evidence that parents were unsatisfied with the industry-sponsored systems. Additionally, the representatives from Harvard and Children Now presented their views on how and why the ratings systems, in general, and the television ratings system, in particular, were inadequate. The MPAA, the TV Parental Guidelines Monitoring Board, and the ESRB stated that they believed the current systems provided the necessary information for parents.

Legislation

On January 14, 2003, Senator Ernest Hollings introduced S. 161, the Children's Protection from Violent Programming Act. That bill contained provisions for the FCC to investigate and report to Congress on the effectiveness of the V-chip and the ratings system and to prohibit the distribution of violent video programming that is not appropriately rated and is therefore not blockable. Additionally, it would have required the Federal Trade Commission to study the marketing of violent content by the motion picture, music recording, and computer and video game industries to children. The bill was referred to the Committee on Science, Commerce, and Transportation the day it was introduced, but no further action was taken; however, the language of this bill was substantially the same as an amendment to S. 2056 (discussed below).

On February 9, 2004, Senator Sam Brownback introduced S. 2056, the Broadcast Decency Enforcement Act. [21] The bill was originally aimed only at increasing the penalties for broadcasters transmitting obscene, indecent, and profane language and, as introduced, contained no reference to the V-chip or the ratings system; the bill was amended on March 9, 2004, during committee mark up by Senators Hollings and Stevens to include language substantially similar to S. 161.

S. 2056 was reported out of the Committee on Commerce, Science, and Transportation and placed on the Senate Legislative Calendar on April 5, 2004. [22] This bill was later added as an amendment to S. 2400, the Ronald Reagan National Defense Authorization Act for FY2005; [23] however, although the amendment was included in the version of the bill passed in the Senate, the language was removed in conference and was not included in the final version of the bill that was signed into law (H.R. 4200). [24]

House of Representatives

During the 108th Congress, the Committee on Energy and Commerce Subcommittee on Telecommunications and the Internet held one hearing that addressed the broader issue of broadcast indecency and one that included a discussion of the V-chip and the ratings system, in particular; one bill specific to the V-chip and the ratings system was introduced.

Hearings

On January 28, 2004, the subcommittee examined the FCC's enforcement policies with respect to broadcast indecency. This hearing was held in response to the FCC's determination in October 2003 that the use of the "f-word" by an artist [25] accepting an award at the Golden Globe Ceremony was not indecent. Four days later, on February 1, 2004, Super Bowl XXXVIII featured a half-time show that included a performance in which one of the entertainer's [26] breasts was revealed. These incidents led to legislation being introduced that would increase the fines for such broadcasts, but specifically related to the V-chip.

On September 13, 2004, the subcommittee held a hearing on the effect of television violence on children. Each of the witnesses presented information about the effects on children of repeated exposure of violent acts. [27] With respect to the Vchip, in particular, Mr. Jeff J. McIntyre of the American Psychological Association, noted that policymakers should be aware that the very industries that develop ratings often continue to market inappropriate materials to minors. For example, a program may be rated as TV-M, but often that same program is marketed to children under 18. [28] On the other hand, Professor Rodney Jay Blackman of the DePaul College of Law, warned against imposing broad restrictions on indecency and instead promoted the use of technology such as the V-chip as an effective tool to control access to unsuitable programming. [29]

Legislation

On March 9, 2005, Representative Joe Baca introduced H.R. 3914, the Children's Protection from Violent Programming Act. This bill was the companion to S. 161 and the two were substantially similar (see discussion above).

The bill was referred to the Committee on Energy and Commerce the day it was introduced and to the Subcommittee on Telecommunications and the Internet on March 11, 2004. No further action was taken.

FEDERAL COMMUNICATIONS COMMISSION ACTION

In July 2004, the FCC initiated a Notice of Inquiry (NOI) to seek comments relating to the "presentation of violent programming and its impact on children." [30] The NOI asked for comments and information regarding trends in the amount of violent programming; the effects of viewing violent programming on children and other segments of the population; whether particular portrayals of violence were more likely to cause deleterious effects than others; whether any further public policymaking should address all violence or just excessive or gratuitous violence; whether the ratings system and the V-chip were accomplishing their intended purpose, or if additional mechanisms needed to be developed to control exposure to media violence; and whether there were legal constraints on either Congress or the Commission to regulate violent programming. [31]

In particular, the FCC requested information on the status of the V-chip and current ratings system as tools to help parents and other viewers screen out violence. With respect to the V-chip, the FCC asked for comments on the overall usefulness of the V-chip, recent initiatives to educate parents about the availability of the Vchip, ways to enhance the usefulness of the V-chip, and whether the mislabeling of violent content described in a recent study could render the V-chip ineffective. With respect to the ratings system, the FCC asked for comments on ways to improve the system, to what extent parents were using it, and whether it provided parents enough information to make educated programming decisions for their children. [32] Comments and replies were due in this proceeding on October 15 and November 15, 2004, respectively. There is no set timetable for further action.

EFFECTIVENESS OF THE V-CHIP: CURRENT RESEARCH

Since 1998, the Kaiser Family Foundation (KFF) has conducted ongoing research into the impact of media violence on children and the effectiveness of the V-chip and television ratings as tools for parents to control access to undesirable television content. [33] In the Foundation's most recent report, "Parents, Media, and Public Policy: A Kaiser Family Foundation Survey," (KFF Study) [34] a majority of parents reported that they were "very" concerned about the amount of sex (60%) and violence

(53%) their children are exposed to on TV. [35]

Overall, the parents interviewed for the study stated that they were more concerned about inappropriate content on TV than in other media: 34% said TV concerned them most, compared to 16% who said the Internet, 10% movies, 7% music, and 5% video games. Half (50%) of all parents said they have used the TV ratings to help guide their children's viewing, including one in four (24%) who said they use them "often." [36]

Furthermore, the study revealed that while use of the V-chip has increased substantially since 2001, when 7% of all parents said they used it, it remains modest at just 15% of all parents, or about four in 10 (42%) of those who have a V-chip in their television and know it. Nearly two-thirds (61%) of parents who have used the V-chip said they found it "very" useful. [37]

Other significant findings reported included:

- After being read arguments on both sides of the issue, nearly two thirds of parents (63%) said they favored new regulations to limit the amount of sex and violence in TV shows during the early evening hours, when children were most likely to be watching (35% are opposed). [38]
- A majority (55%) of parents said ratings should be displayed more prominently and 57% said they would rather keep the current rating systems than switch to a single rating for TV, movies, video games, and music (34% favor the single rating). [39]
- When read the competing arguments for subjecting cable TV to the same content standards as broadcasters, half of all parents (52%) said that cable should be treated the same, while 43% said it should not. [40]
- Most parents who have used the TV ratings said they found them either "very" (38%) or "somewhat" (50%) useful. [41]
- About half (52%) of all parents said most TV shows are rated accurately, while about four in ten (39%) said most are not. [42]
- Many parents do not understand what the various ratings guidelines mean. For example, 28% of parents of young children (2-6 years old) knew what the rating TV-Y7 meant (directed to children age 7 and older) while 13% thought it meant the opposite (directed to children under 7); and only 12% knew that the rating FV ("fantasy violence") is related to violent content, while 8% thought it meant "family viewing." [43]

In releasing the survey results, Vicky Rideout, Vice President and Director of the Kaiser Family Foundation's Program for the Study of

Entertainment Media and Health, commented, "While many parents have used the ratings or the V-Chip, too many still don't know what the ratings mean or even that their TV includes a VChip." [44]

A number of groups conducted research and published opinion pieces questioning the usefulness and/or legality of the V-chip and the ratings system after the 1996 Telecommunications Act was enacted (e.g., the American Civil Liberties Union, Cato Institute, Morality in Media). Since that time, opposition has waned and even the recent controversies did not renew it. Further, while the V-chip and the ratings system can block objectionable or indecent programming when used in tandem, since the incidents were broadcast "live" and did not have ratings that would have blocked them, neither the V-chip nor the ratings system would have been effective in either case. Therefore, some could claim that the V-chip and the ratings system, while useful tools in many cases, remain unreliable tools for parents because they cannot guarantee all objectionable content will be blocked.

ISSUES FOR CONGRESS

Congress may wish to consider a number of possible options to support parents in monitoring and controlling their children's access to certain programming. Some of these options would require only further educational outreach to parents, while others would require at least regulatory, if not legislative action.

Awareness of the V-Chip and the Ratings System

According the 2004 KFF Study, parents also indicated that they would like to see the ratings displayed more prominently to make it easier to notice them. Such findings are consistent with a lack of wide-spread usage or even awareness of the Vchip. Specifically, as noted above, the 2004 KFF study indicated that even after years of being available, only 42% of parents who have a V-chip and are aware of it actually use it. However, of the parents that had used the V-chip, 89% found it "somewhat" to "very" useful. [45] Those figures would indicate that increased knowledge of the V-chip would substantially increase parents' perceptions of control over their children's television viewing.

One of the easiest approaches to increasing the use of the V-chip may likely be to step up parental awareness programs through, for example, public service announcements on television, educational materials on the FCC website, and possibly pubic service advertisements in print media. Additionally, such educational materials could be made available on Congressional Member websites for constituents to download. Such actions would not require any new legislation or additional work by the ratings board or related entities; however, some initially may require funding.

Media-Specific vs. Uniform Ratings

One of the ongoing issues related to the use of the V-chip is that, according to the KFF study, only about half of parents actually use the television ratings. That is low in comparison with the movie ratings, which are used by approximately 78% of parents, but in line with the use of ratings for music and video games. [46] One contributor to the low use of the ratings is likely that so few parents actually understand the ratings. For example, as stated earlier, only 12% of parents of young children knew that "FV" is the rating for Fantasy Violence; further, 8% believed it to mean "Family Viewing." As noted by the researchers in their report, the FV rating "is the only rating that denotes anything about the violent content of children's programming, one of the impetuses for the development of the ratings system" in the first place. Finally, overall, 20% of parents had never even heard of the ratings system. [47]

In light of those figures, it could appear that parents might prefer a single, unified ratings system that would be applied across different media. However, while 34% of parents said they would prefer a unified system, 57% opposed a unified system. [48] Given the overall findings by KFF regarding parents' knowledge and use of the ratings system, there appears to be enough ambiguity on this issue to warrant further investigation by Congress.

Independent Ratings Systems and an "Open" V-Chip

Under current legislative and regulatory mandates, the V-chip is only required to "read" the TV Parental Guidelines and the MPAA (movie) Ratings. This means that any independent system can only be used to augment parental knowledge, not to program the V-chip. So, while a range of varied, independent ratings systems can serve to provide additional information to parents, they cannot be used with the current closed V-chip technology. In order for these ratings to become as useful as possible, the V-chip would have to be able to read them.

The opportunity to encourage the further development of private ratings systems exists in the transition to digital television. Beginning in April 2005, all broadcasters must simulcast 100 percent of their National Television System Committee (commonly referred to as "NTSC") programming on their digital channel; by the end of 2006, broadcasters must turn off their analog signal. [49] Through either regulatory (i.e., FCC) or legislative action, television manufacturers could be required to install an open V-chip that could be reprogrammed to read altered or even completely new ratings. An "open" V-chip requirement would allow changes to the current system to be read as well as accommodate any other ratings system(s). This issue is currently under consideration at the FCC. [50]

ENDNOTES

[1] "Parents, Media, and Public Policy: A Kaiser Family Foundation Survey," Kaiser Family Foundation, Fall 2004, p. 2. Available online at [http://www.kff.org/entmedia/ entmedia092304pkg.cfm]. (KFF Study)

[2] KFF Study, p. 2. Specifically, 63% said they were ""very concerned" and 26% said they were "somewhat concerned."

[3] Telecommunications Act of 1996, P.L. 104-104, February 8, 1996, available online at [http://www.fcc.gov/Reports/ 1934new.pdf]. The 1996 Act amended the Communications Act of 1934 (47 U.S.C. 101, *et seq.*), updating some existing sections and adding new sections to account for new technologies. One such addition to the law was to mandate the inclusion of a computer chip in new television sets to allow parents more control over the programming viewed by their children (47 U.S.C. 303 (x)). The 1934 Act, as amended by the 1996 Act, is available online at [http://www.fcc.gov/Reports/tcom1996.pdf].

[4] Although commonly believed to be short for "violence," the V in V-chip is actually short for "ViewControl," the name given by the inventor of the device. See "V-Chip Technology Invented by Professor Tim Col l i n g s ," available online at [http://www.tri-vision.ca/documents/Collings%20As%20Inventor.pdf]. See also, "The History of Invention," available online at

[http://www.cbc.ca/kids/general/the-lab/history-of-invention/vchip.html].

[5] The ratings data are sent on line 21 of the Vertical Blanking Interval found in the National Television System Committee (NTSC) signals used for U.S. television broadcasting.

[6] This report focuses on the use of the V-chip and the ratings system as a tool to assist parents in selecting appropriate television programming for their children. However, both the V-chip and the ratings system can be used by a wide range of viewers, from individuals who, themselves, do not wish to view content they find objectionable to individuals who may be babysitting on an intermittent basis in their homes. Further, the V-chip and the television ratings are closely related to another issue — that of broadcast indecency and how to define and enforce the appropriate use of the public airwaves by the television media. That issue is discussed in greater detail in CRS Report RL32222, "Regulation of Broadcast Indecency: Background and Legal Analysis," by Angie A. Welborn and Henry Cohen.

[7] 47 U.S.C. 303 (x).

[8] 47 U.S.C. 303 (w)(1).

[9] The group included the national broadcast networks; independent, affiliated and public television stations; cable programmers; producers and distributors of cable programming; entertainment and movie studios; and members of the guilds representing writers, directors, producers and actors.

[10] As of January 1, 2000, all new television sets with a picture screen 13 inches or greater sold in the United States must be equipped with the V-chip.

[11] H.Res. 482 (Expressing the sense of the House of Representatives with respect to the October 3, 2003, order released by the Federal Communications Commission's Enforcement Bureau in response to complaints regarding the broadcast of program material that contained indecent language); H.Res. 500 (Expressing the sense of the House of Representatives that the Federal Communications Commission should vigorously enforce indecency and profanity laws pursuant to the intent of Congress in order to protect children in the United States from indecent and profane programming on broadcast television and radio); H.Res. 554 (Providing for consideration of H.R. 3717 to increase the penalties for violations by television and radio broadcasters of the prohibitions against transmission of obscene,

indecent, and profane language), passed in the House March 11, 2004; and S.Res. 283 (A resolution affirming the need to protect children in the United States from indecent programming), passed in the Senate on December 9, 2003.

[12] A number of bills were introduced related to increasing fines for violating rules on indecent programming, but that issue is outside the scope of this report. For more information, please refer to CRS Report "Regulation of Broadcast Indecency: Background and Legal Analysis," by Angie A. Welborn and Henry Cohen, available online at [http://www.congress.gov/erp/rl/pdf/RL32222.pdf].

[13] As discussed in this section, S. 161 was the only bill that contained reference to the Vchip and the ratings system as introduced. S. 2056 was amended in committee to include language that was substantially the same as that contained in S. 161.

[14] The MPAA represents the motion picture industry. See the MPAA website online at [http://www.mpaa.org].

[15] The ESRB represents the video gaming industry. See the ESRB website online at [http://www.esrb.org].

[16] See the Kids Risk website online at [http://www.kidsrisk.harvard.edu].

[17] See the Children and the Media Program website online at [http://www.childrennow.org/media].

[18] PSV Ratings is a for-profit company that produces independent ratings. See the PSV Ratings website online at [http://www.psvratings.com].

[19] As noted earlier, the TV Parental Guidelines Monitoring Board assigns ratings to television programming, except news and sports. The board has a chairman and six members each from the broadcast television industry, the cable industry, and the program production community. The chairman also selects five non-industry members from the advocacy community, for a total of 24 members. See the board's website for additional information, [http://www.tvguidelines.org/default.asp].

[20] Independent ratings systems are produced by both for-profit and not-for-profit entities.

[21] Although H.R. 3717 was considered the companion bill to S. 2056, it was never amended to include any reference to the V-chip and ratings system.

[22] See Report of the Committee on Commerce, Science, and Transportation on S. 2056, the Broadcast Decency Enforcement Act

of 2004, House Report 108-253, April 5, 2004. Available online at [http://frwebgate.access.gpo.gov/cgi-bin/getdoc.cgi?dbname=108_cong_reports&docid=f:sr253.108.pdf].

[23] S. 2400, the Ronald Reagan National Defense Authorization Act for FY2005, as passed by the Senate, sections 1085-1087.

[24] Conference Report to Accompany H.R. 4200, the Ronald W. Reagan National Defense Authorization Act for Fiscal Year 2005, Conference Report 108-767, October 8, 2004, p. 797. Available online at [http://frwebgate.access.gpo.gov/cgi-bin/getdoc.cgi?dbname=108_cong_reports&docid=f:hr767.108.pdf].

[25] Bono of the rock band U2.

[26] Janet Jackson.

[27] A full list of witnesses with links to their testimony can be found online at [http://energycommerce.house.gov/108/Hearings/09132004hearing1355/hearing.htm].

[28] Testimony of Jeff J. McIntyre, Senior Legislative and Federal Affairs Officer, Public Policy Office, American Psychological Association, available online at [http://energycommerce.house.gov/108/Hearings/09132004hearing1355/McIntyre2197.htm].

[29] Testimony of Professor Rodney Jay Blackman, DePaul College of Law, available online at [http://energycommerce.house.gov/108/Hearings/09132004hearing1355/Blackman2200.htm].

[30] *In the Matter of Violent Television Programming and its Impact on Children* (MB Docket 04-175), Notice of Inquiry (NOI), Adopted July 15, 2004; Released July 28, 2004. The NOI is available online at [http://hraunfoss.fcc.gov/edocs_public/attachmatch/FCC-04-175A1.pdf].

[31] NOI, para. 2.

[32] NOI, paras. 16-19.See also NOI, para 22.

[33] See Kaiser Family Foundation, Program on Study of Entertainment Media & Health: Television/Video, [http://www.kff.org/entmedia/tv.cfm].

[34] "Parents, Media, and Public Policy: A Kaiser Family Foundation Survey," Kaiser Family Foundation, Fall 2004 (KFF Study). The survey of 1,001 parents of children ages 2-17 was conducted in July and August 2004.

[35] KFF Study, p. 3.

[36] KFF Study, p. 2.

[37] KFF Study, p. 7.

[38] KFF Study, p. 8.
[39] Ibid.
[40] Ibid.
[41] KFF Study, p. 5.
[42] Ibid.
[43] KFF Study, p. 6.
[44] KFF News Release, "Parents Favor New Limits on TV Content in Early Evening Hours; Half of Parents Say Cable TV Should Adhere to Same Standards as Broadcast TV; Use of the V-Chip is Up," September 23, 2004. Available online at [http://www.kff.org/entmedia/ entmedia092304nr.cfm].
[45] KFF Study, p. 7.
[46] KFF Study, p. 4.
[47] KFF Study, p. 6.
[48] KFF Study, p. 8.
[49] The December 31, 2006, deadline may be extended under a number of circumstances, detailed in CRS Report RL31260, Digital Television: An Overview, by Lennard Kruger.
[50] *In the Matter of Second Periodic Review of the Commission's Rules and Policies Affecting the Conversion To Digital Television*, MB Docket No. 03-15, RM 9832, Report and Order, September 4, 2004, paras. 154-159. Available online at [http://hraunfoss.fcc.gov/edocs_public/attachmatch/FCC-04-192A1.pdf]. One issue that remains under consideration involves new language concerning the V-chip and how it will be incorporated into digital television sets. The Consumer Electronics Association filed a petition to change the language that the FCC adopted in the Order. That petition is available online at [http://hraunfoss.fcc.gov/edocs_public/attachmatch/DA-03-1292A1.pdf]. The opposition to CEA's Petition for Reconsideration by Tri-Vision (the inventor of the V-chip) is available online at [http://www.tri-vision.ca/documents/ 2004/FCC%20Tri-vision%20Opposition.pdf]. See also *In the Matter of Children's Television Obligations of Digital Television Broadcasters*, MM Docket No. 00-167, Report and Order and Further Notice of Proposed Rulemaking, November 23, 2004, paras. 62-65. Available online at [http://hraunfoss.fcc.gov/edocs_public/attachmatch/FCC-04-221A1.pdf].

Chapter 3

OBSCENITY AND INDECENCY: CONSTITUTIONAL PRINCIPLES AND FEDERAL STATUTES[*]

Henry Cohen

PREFACE

The First Amendment provides: "Congress shall make no law . . . abridging the freedom of speech, or of the press." In general, the First Amendment protects pornography, with this term being used to mean any erotic material. The Supreme Court, however, has held that the First Amendment does not protect two types of pornography: obscenity and child pornography. Consequently, they may be banned on the basis of their content, and federal law prohibits the mailing of obscenity, as well as its transport or receipt in interstate or foreign commerce.

Most pornography is not legally obscene; to be obscene, pornography must, at a minimum, "depict or describe patently offensive 'hard core' sexual conduct." The Supreme Court has created a three-part test, known as the *Miller* test, to determine whether a work is obscene. Pornography that is not obscene may not be banned, but may be regulated as to the time, place, and manner of its distribution, particularly in order to keep it from children. Thus, the courts have upheld the zoning and licensing of pornography dealers, as well as restrictions on dial-a-porn, nude dancing, and indecent

---

[*] Excerpted from CRS Report 95-804 A dated June 25, 2003

radio and television broadcasting.

Federal statutes, in addition to making it a crime to mail obscenity or to transport or receive it in interstate or foreign commerce, provide for criminal and civil forfeiture of real and personal property used in making obscenity pornography, and of the profits of obscenity – in some instances even when they were already used to pay a third party. In addition, obscenity crimes are included among the predicate offenses that may give rise to a violation of the Federal Racketeer Influenced and Corrupt Organizations Act (RICO).

The Internet has given rise to three federal statutes designed to protect minors from sexual material posted on it. The Communications Decency Act of 1996 makes it a crime knowingly to use a telecommunications device (telephone, fax, or e-mail) to make an obscene or indecent communication to a minor, or knowingly to use an interactive computer service to transmit an obscene communication to anyone or an indecent communication to a minor. The Supreme Court, however, held the inclusion of "indecent" communications in this statute unconstitutional. Congress, in response, enacted the less-broad Child Online Protection Act (COPA), the enforcement of which has been enjoined while its constitutionality is being challenged. Finally, the Children's Internet Protection Act (CIPA), enacted at the end of the 106th Congress, requires schools and libraries that accept federal funds to purchase computers or Internet access to block or filter obscenity, child pornography, and, with respect to minors, material that is "harmful to minors." Filters may be disabled, however, "for bona fide research or other lawful purpose." On June 23, 2003, the Supreme Court held CIPA constitutional.

Constitutional Principles

To be constitutional, a federal statute must be enacted pursuant to a power of Congress enumerated in the Constitution and must not contravene any provision of the Constitution. Two powers enumerated in Article I, Section 8 of the Constitution give Congress the power to enact statutes regulating or banning pornography: the power "To regulate Commerce with foreign Nations, and among the several States," and the power "To establish Post Offices and post Roads." Thus, Congress may enact statutes, provided they do not contravene any provision of the Constitution, that regulate pornography that crosses state or national boundaries, is imported or exported, or is mailed.

The provision of the Constitution that federal statutes regulating pornography are most likely to be in danger of contravening is the First Amendment's provision that "Congress shall make no law . . . abridging the freedom of speech, or of the press." [1] Although pornography in general is protected by the First Amendment, two types of pornography – obscenity and child pornography – are not. [2] Therefore, pornography that does not constitute obscenity or child pornography may ordinarily be regulated only with respect to its time, place, and manner of distribution. [3] An outright ban on pornography other than obscenity or child pornography would violate the First Amendment unless it served "to promote a compelling interest" and was "the least restrictive means to further the articulated interest." [4] Obscenity and child pornography, however, being without First Amendment protection, may be totally banned on the basis of their content, not only in the absence of a compelling governmental interest, but in the absence of any evidence of harm.

Obscenity apparently is unique in being the only type of speech to which the Supreme Court has denied First Amendment protection without regard to whether it can cause harm. According to the Court, there is evidence that, at the time of the adoption of the First Amendment, obscenity "was outside the protection intended for speech and press." [5] Consequently, obscenity may be banned simply because a legislature concludes that banning it protects "the social interest in order and morality." [6]

A. The Miller Test

Most pornography is not legally obscene; *i.e.*, most pornography is protected by the First Amendment. To be obscene, pornography must, at a minimum, "depict or describe patently offensive 'hard core' sexual conduct." [7] The Supreme Court has created a three-part test, known as the *Miller* test, to determine whether a work is obscene. The *Miller* test asks:

> (a) whether the "average person applying contemporary community standards" would find that the work, taken as a whole, appeals to the prurient interest; (b) whether the work depicts or describes, in a patently offensive way, sexual conduct specifically defined by the applicable state law; and (c) whether the work, taken as a whole, lacks serious literary, artistic, political, or scientific value. [8]

In *Pope v. Illinois*, the Supreme Court clarified that "the first and second prongs of the *Miller* test—appeal to prurient interest and patent offensiveness—are issues of fact for the jury to determine applying contemporary community standards." [9] However, as for the third prong, "[t]he proper inquiry is not whether an ordinary member of any given community would find serious literary, artistic, political, or scientific value in allegedly obscene material, but whether a reasonable person would find such value in the material, taken as a whole." [10]

When a federal statute refers to "obscenity," it should be understood to refer only to pornography that is obscene under the *Miller* standard, as application of the statute to other material would ordinarily be unconstitutional. [11] However, narrowly drawn statutes that serve a compelling interest, such as protecting minors, may be permissible even if they restrict pornography that is not obscene under *Miller*. [12] In *Sable Communications of California, Inc. v. Federal Communications Commission*, the Supreme Court

> recognized that there is a compelling interest in protecting the physical and psychological well-being of minors. This interest extends to shielding minors from the influence of literature that is not obscene by adult standards. The government may serve this legitimate interest, but to withstand constitutional scrutiny, "it must do so by narrowly drawn regulations without unnecessarily interfering with First Amendment freedoms." It is not enough to show that the government's ends are compelling; the means must be carefully tailored to achieved those ends. [13]

In *Sable*, the Supreme Court applied these principles to the government's attempt to proscribe dial-a-porn; see, page 10, below.

The Supreme Court has allowed one exception to the rule that obscenity, as defined by *Miller*, is not protected under the First Amendment. In *Stanley v. Georgia*, the Court held that "mere private possession of obscene material" is protected. The Court wrote:

> Whatever may be the justifications for other statutes regulating obscenity, we do not think they reach into the privacy of one's own home. If the First Amendment means anything, it means that a State has no business telling a man, sitting alone in his house, what books he may read or what films he may watch. [14]

Subsequently, however, the Supreme Court rejected the claim that under *Stanley* there is a constitutional right to provide obscene material for private use, [15] or to acquire it for private use. [16] The right to possess obscene material does not imply the right to provide or acquire it, because the right to possess it "reflects no more than . . . the law's 'solicitude to protect the privacies of the life within [the home].'" [17]

B. Zoning and Licensing of Pornography Dealers

In *Young v. American Mini Theaters, Inc.*, the Supreme Court held that "[t]he mere fact that the commercial exploitation of material protected by the First Amendment is subject to zoning and other licensing requirements is not a sufficient reason for invalidating these ordinances." [18] In *Young*, the Court upheld ordinances that required dispersal of "adult" establishments; specifically, the ordinances provided that an adult theater could not be located within 1,000 feet of any two other "regulated uses" (adult bookstores, cabarets, bars, hotels, etc.) or within 500 feet of a residential area. In *Renton v. Playtime Theaters, Inc.*, the Court upheld an ordinance that required that adult theaters be concentrated in limited areas; it prohibited adult "theaters from locating within 1,000 feet of any residential zone, single or multiple-family dwelling, church, park, or school." [19]

In *Young*, the Court reasoned that

> what is ultimately at stake is nothing more than a limitation on the place where adult films may be exhibited, even though the determination of whether a particular film fits that characterization turns on the nature of its content. . . . The situation would be quite different if the ordinance had the effect of suppressing, or greatly restricting access to, lawful speech. [20]

In *Renton*, the Court wrote:

> The ordinance by its terms is designed to prevent crime, protect the city's retail trade, maintain property values, and generally "protec[t] and preserv[e] the quality of [the city's] neighborhoods, commercial districts, and the quality of urban life," not to suppress the expression of unpopular views. . . . In short, the Renton ordinance is completely consistent with our definition of "content neutral" speech regulations as those that "are *justified* without reference to the content of the regulated speech." [21]

In both *Young* and *Renton*, the Court found the ordinances in question to be narrow enough to affect only those theaters shown to produce the unwanted secondary effects, such as crime. [22] In this respect they were unlike the regulations the Court struck down as overbroad in two other cases. In *Erznoznik v. City of Jacksonville*, the ordinance prohibited drive-in theaters from showing films containing nudity when the screen was visible from a public street. [23] In *Schad v. Mount Ephraim*, the ordinance prohibited live entertainment from a broad range of commercial uses permitted in a commercial zone; the ordinance in this case was used to prosecute an adult bookstore that featured coin-operated booths that permitted customers to watch nude dancing. [24]

In *FW/PBS, Inc. v. Dallas*, the Supreme Court considered a challenge to a city ordinance that regulated "sexually oriented businesses through a scheme incorporating zoning, licensing, and inspections," and prohibited "individuals convicted of certain crimes from obtaining a license to operate a sexually oriented business for a specified period of years." [25] The ordinance defined a "sexually oriented business" as "an adult arcade, adult bookstore or adult video store, adult cabaret, adult motel, adult motion picture theater, escort agency, nude model studio, or sexual encounter center." [26] The Court held that the licensing scheme

> does not provide for an effective limitation on the time within which the licensor's decision must be made. It also fails to provide an avenue for prompt judicial review so as to minimize suppression of the speech in the event of a license denial. We therefore hold that the failure to provide these essential safeguards renders the ordinance's licensing requirement unconstitutional insofar as it is enforced against those businesses engaged in First Amendment activity.... [27]

One type of business covered by the ordinance that was not engaged in First Amendment activity was adult motels, which the ordinance defined as motels that rented rooms for less than 10 hours. Inclusion of these motels was challenged on two grounds: (1) that the city had "violated the Due Process Clause by failing to produce adequate support for its supposition that renting rooms for less than 10 hours results in increased crime or other secondary effects," and (2) "that the 10-hour limitation on the rental of motel rooms places an unconstitutional burden on the right to freedom of association...." [28]

The Court rejected both arguments. As for the first, it found "it reasonable to believe that shorter rental time periods indicate that the motels foster prostitution." [29] As for the second, it found that the associations "that are formed from the use of a motel room for less than 10 hours are not those that have 'played a critical role in the culture and traditions of the Nation by cultivating and transmitting shared ideals and beliefs.'" [30]

In *Los Angeles v. Alameda Books, Inc.*, the Supreme Court reversed a grant of summary judgment that had struck down a municipal ordinance that prohibited "the establishment or maintenance of more than one adult entertainment business in the same building, structure or portion thereof." [31] A federal district court had granted summary judgment and the Court of Appeals for the Ninth Circuit had affirmed on the ground "that the city failed to present evidence upon which it could reasonably rely to demonstrate a link between multiple-use adult establishments and negative secondary effects." [32] The Supreme Court reversed, finding that "[t]he city of Los Angeles may reasonably rely on a study it conducted some years before enacting the present version of § 12.70(C) to demonstrate that its ban on multiple-use adult establishments serves its interest in reducing crime." [33] It therefore remanded the case so that the city would have the opportunity to demonstrate this at trial.

The four-judge plurality opinion in *Alameda Books* "held that a municipality may rely on any evidence that is 'reasonably believed to be relevant' for demonstrating a causal connection between speech and a substantial, independent governmental interest," such as reducing crime or maintaining property values. [34] Justice Kennedy, whose concurring opinion was necessary for a majority, added that, not only must the city demonstrate that its ordinance "has the purpose and effect of suppressing secondary effects"; it must also demonstrate that it will leave "the quantity and accessibility of speech substantially intact." [35] The four dissenting justices found that "the city has failed to show any causal relationship between the breakup policy and elimination or regulation of secondary effects," and, therefore, that summary judgment had been properly granted. [36]

C. Nude Dancing

The Supreme Court has twice upheld the application of laws banning public nudity to nudity in "adult" entertainment establishments where the viewers are all consenting adults who have paid to see the dancers. In *Barnes v. Glen Theatre, Inc.*, the Supreme Court held that the First Amendment does not prevent the government from requiring that dancers wear "pasties" and a "G-string" when they dance (nonobscenely) in such establishments. [37] Indiana sought to enforce a state statute prohibiting public nudity against two such establishments, which asserted First Amendment protection. The Court found that the statute proscribed public nudity across the board, not nude dancing as such, and therefore imposed only an incidental restriction on expression. A statute that is intended to suppress speech will be upheld only if it serves a compelling governmental interest and is the least restrictive means to further that interest. By contrast, under *United States v.O'Brien*, a statute that imposes an incidental restriction, like one that imposes a time, place, or manner restriction, will be upheld if it is narrowly tailored to further a substantial, but not necessarily compelling, governmental interest. [38]

There was no majority opinion in the case. Justice Rehnquist, joined by Justices O'Connor and Kennedy, found the statute no more restrictive than necessary to further the governmental interest of "protecting societal order and morality." [39]

Justice Souter found the relevant governmental interest to be "combating the secondary effects of adult entertainment establishments," such as prostitution, sexual assaults, and other criminal activity. [40] The fifth Justice necessary to uphold the nude dancing prohibition, Justice Scalia, thought that the case raised no First Amendment issue at all, because the incidental restriction was on conduct, not speech, and "virtually *every* law restricts conduct, and virtually *any* prohibited conduct can be performed for expressive purposes." [41] Four Justices dissented, finding insufficient "the plurality and Justice Scalia's simple references to the State's general interest in promoting societal order and morality . . . . The purpose of forbidding people to appear nude in parks, beaches, hot dog stands, and like public places is to protect others from offense. But that could not possibly be the purpose of preventing nude dancing in theaters and barrooms since the viewers are exclusively consenting adults who paid money to see these dances. The purpose of the proscription in these contexts is to protect the viewers from what the State believes is the harmful message that nude dancing communicates." [42] This purpose is impermissible under the First Amendment.

In *Erie v. Pap's A.M.*, the Supreme Court again upheld the application of a statute prohibiting public nudity to an "adult" entertainment establishment. [43] Although there was again only a plurality opinion, this time by Justice O'Connor, Parts I and II of that opinion were joined by five justices. These five adopted Justice Souter's position in *Barnes*, that the statute satisfied the *O'Brien* test because it was intended "to combat harmful secondary effects," such as "prostitution and other criminal activity." [44] Justice Souter, however, though joining the plurality opinion, also dissented in part in *Erie*. He continued to believe that secondary effects were an adequate justification for banning nude dancing, but did not believe "that the city has made a sufficient evidentiary showing to sustain its regulation," and therefore would have remanded the case for further proceedings. [45] He acknowledged his "mistake" in *Barnes* in failing to make the same demand for evidence. [46]

The plurality opinion in *Erie* found that the effect of Erie's public nudity ban "on the erotic message . . . is *de minimis*" because Erie allows dancers to perform wearing only pasties and G-strings. [47] It may follow that "requiring dancers to wear pasties and G-strings may not greatly reduce . . . secondary effects, but *O'Brien* requires only that the regulation further the interest of combating such effects," not that it further it to a particular extent. [48] Justice Scalia, this time joined by Justice Thomas, again took the view that, "[w]hen conduct other than speech itself is regulated . . . the First Amendment is violated only '[w]here the government prohibits conduct precisely because of its communicative attributes." [49] He found, therefore, that the statute should be upheld without regard to "secondary effects," but simply as an attempt "to foster good morals." [50]

Justice Stevens, dissenting in *Erie* and joined by Justice Ginsburg, wrote: "Until now, the 'secondary effects' of commercial enterprises featuring indecent entertainment have justified only the regulation of their location. For the first time, the Court has now held that such effects may justify the total suppression of protected speech. Indeed, the plurality opinion concludes that admittedly trivial advancements of a State's interest may provide the basis for censorship." [51] It concludes, that is, that the *O'Brien* "test can be satisfied by nothing more than the mere possibility of *de minimis* effects on the neighborhood." [52]

The plurality in *Erie* did not address the question of whether statutes prohibiting public nudity could be applied to ban serious theater that contains nudity. In *Barnes*, Justice Souter wrote: "It is difficult to see . . . how the enforcement of Indiana's statute against nudity in a production of 'Hair' or 'Equus' somewhere other than an 'adult' theater would further the State's interest in avoiding harmful secondary effects . . . ." [53]

Federal Obscenity and Indecency Statutes

A. Postal Service Provisions

Sections 3008 and 3010 of Title 39 allow people to prevent mail that they find offensive from being sent to them. Section 3008 provides that a person who receives in the mail "any pandering advertisement which offers for sale matter which the addressee in his sole discretion believes to be erotically arousing or sexually provocative" may request the Postal Service to issue an order directing the sender to refrain from further mailings to the addressee, and the Postal Service must do so. If the Postal Service believes that a sender has violated such an order, it may request the Attorney General to apply to a federal court for an order directing compliance.

The language of 39 U.S.C. § 3008 is broad enough to apply to any unwanted advertisement, regardless of content, as the Supreme Court indicated in upholding the constitutionality of the statute. "We. . . categorically reject," the Court said, "the argument that a vendor has a right under the Constitution or otherwise to send unwanted material into the home of another." [54]

Section 3010 provides that any person may file with the Postal Service a statement "that he desires to receive no sexually oriented advertisements through the mails." The Postal Service shall make the list available, and "[n]o person shall mail or cause to be mailed any sexually oriented advertisement to any individual whose name and address has been on the list for more than 30 days." Section 3011 provides that, if the Postal Service believes that any person is violating section 3010, it may request the Attorney General to commence a civil action against such person in a federal district court. The court may employ various remedies to prevent future mailings.

Violations of sections 3008 and 3010 are also subject to criminal penalties under 18 U.S.C. § 1737.

B. Dial-a-Porn

The federal law concerning dial-a-porn is section 223(b) of the Communications Act of 1934, as amended, 47 U.S.C. § 223(b). Prior to April 1988, it banned both obscene and indecent dial-a-porn in interstate commerce and foreign communications, but only if it involved persons under eighteen. Although pornography that is indecent but not obscene is protected by the First Amendment, restricting minors' access to pornography, even to non-obscene pornography, generally presents no constitutional problems, as minors do not have the same rights as adults under the First Amendment.

Therefore, the pre-April 1988 version of section 223(b) apparently was constitutional. In April 1988, however, P.L. 100-297, § 6101, amended section 223(b) to ban obscene and indecent dial-a-porn in interstate and foreign communications, whether involving adults or children.

In June 1989, the Supreme Court declared section 223(b) unconstitutional insofar as it applies to indecent messages that are not obscene. [55] The Court noted "that while the Government has a legitimate interest in protecting children from exposure to indecent dial-a-porn messages, § 223(b) was not sufficiently narrowly drawn to serve that purpose and thus violated the First Amendment." [56] "[C]redit card, access code, and scrambling rules . . . [would have] represented a 'feasible and effective' way to serve the Government's compelling interest in protecting children." [57] The government argued that these methods "would not be effective enough," but the Court found "no evidence in the record . . . to that effect . . . ." [58]

The Court concluded:

> Because the statute's denial of adult access to telephone messages which are indecent but not obscene far exceeds that which is necessary to limit the access of minors to such messages, we hold that the ban does not survive constitutional scrutiny. [59]

The upshot of *Sable* was that Congress' 1988 extension to adults of the ban on dial-a-porn that is indecent but not obscene resulted in federal law's not banning such dial-a-porn at all, even if used by minors. Section 223(b) after the decision banned dial-a-porn only if it was obscene.

Therefore, in 1989, Congress enacted P.L. 101-166, known as the "Helms Amendment," which amended section 223(b) to ban indecent dial-a-porn, if used by persons under 18. Under the 1988 law, section 223(b) applied "in the District of Columbia or in interstate or foreign communications"; under the Helms Amendment, it applies to all calls "within the United States." The Helms Amendment also added section 223(c), which prohibits telephone companies, "to the extent technically feasible," from providing access to any dial-a-porn "from the telephone of any subscriber who has not previously requested [it] in writing . . . ." In order to enable telephone companies to comply with this provision, Federal

Communications Commission regulations require dial-a-porn providers to give written notice to the telephone company that they are providing indecent communications. 47 C.F.R. § 64.201. [60]

The Helms Amendment was challenged as unconstitutional, but a federal court of appeals upheld it, and the Supreme Court declined to review the case. [61] The court of appeals found that the word "indecent" as used in the statute was not void for vagueness, [62] that the statute was the least restrictive means to achieve a compelling governmental interest, [63] and that the requirement that the dial-a-porn provider inform the telephone company that its message was indecent did not constitute prior restraint.

C. Obscenity Provisions at 18 U.S.C. §§ 1460-1470

Federal law contains no outright ban on all obscenity; it leaves this to state law.

However, the following federal statutes prohibit, among other things, obscenity on federal land or in federal buildings, in the mail, on radio and television, in interstate or foreign commerce, and on interstate highways and railroads even when the obscene material is transported intrastate.

Section 1460

This section makes it a crime, "in the special maritime and territorial jurisdiction of the United States or on any land or building owned by, leased to, or otherwise used by or under the control of the Government of the United States," or "in the Indian country as defined in section 1151 of this title," to sell or to possess with intent to sell, any obscene visual depiction.

Section 1461

This section declares to be "nonmailable matter" any" obscene, lewd, lascivious, indecent, filthy, or vile article, matter, thing, device, or substance," and makes it a crime knowingly to mail nonmailable matter. This statute should be read to prohibit only what constitutionally may be prohibited. [64]

Section 1462

This section prohibits importation of, and interstate or foreign transportation of, "any obscene, lewd, lascivious, or filthy" printed matter, film, or sound recording, "or other matter of indecent character." The

Supreme Court has written that, if and when serious doubt is raised as to the vagueness of the terms used in section 1462,

> we are prepared to construe such terms as limiting regulated material to patently offensive representations or descriptions of that specific "hard core" sexual conduct given as examples in *Miller* v. *California, ante,* at 25. . . . Of course, Congress could always define other specific "hard core" conduct. [65]

In 1996, P.L. 104-104, § 507(a), amended 18 U.S.C. § 1462 to apply to any "interactive computer service."

Section 1463

This section prohibits mailing matter, "upon the envelope or outside cover or wrapper of which, and all postal cards, upon which, any delineations, epithets, terms, or language of an indecent, lewd, lascivious, or obscene character are written or printed or otherwise impressed or apparent." Under this provision, "language of an 'indecent' character must be equated with language of an 'obscene' character" (and does not include "writing [on a post card] that a female runs around a dwelling house naked"). [66]

Section 1464

This section provides, in full: Whoever utters any obscene, indecent, or profane language by means of radio communication shall be fined under this title or imprisoned not more than two years, or both. [67]

This statute, unlike the others cited thus far, may be applied to language that is not obscene under *Miller*. This is because broadcasting has more limited First Amendment protection than other media. As the Supreme Court explained in *Red Lion Broadcasting Co. v. Federal Communications Commission*:

> Where there are substantially more individuals who want to broadcast than there are frequencies to allocate, it is idle to posit an unabridgeable First Amendment right to broadcast comparable to the right of every individual to speak, write, or publish. [68]

In *Federal Communications Commission v. Pacifica Foundation,* the FCC had taken action against a radio station for broadcasting a recording of George Carlin's "Filthy Words" monologue at 2 p.m., and the station had claimed First Amendment protection. [69] The Supreme Court upheld the power of the FCC under § 1464 "to regulate a radio broadcast that is indecent but not obscene." [70] The Court cited two distinctions between broadcasting and other media: "First, the broadcast media have established a uniquely pervasive presence in the lives of all Americans . . . confront[ing] the citizen, not only in public, but also in the privacy of the home . . . ," and "Second, broadcasting is uniquely accessible to children . . . ." [71]

Nevertheless, the broadcast media have some First Amendment protection, and the Court emphasized the narrowness of its holding:

> The Commission's decision rested entirely on a nuisance rationale under which context is all-important. The concept requires consideration of a host of variables. The time of day was emphasized by the Commission. . . . [72]

Furthermore, the Commission "never intended to place an absolute prohibition on the broadcast of this type of language, but rather sought to channel it to times of day when children most likely would not be exposed to it." [73]

In 1988, Congress enacted P.L. 100-459, § 608, which required the FCC to promulgate regulations to ban indecent broadcasts 24 hours a day. The FCC did so, but the regulations never took effect because the court of appeals declared the ban unconstitutional because "the Commission may not ban such broadcasts entirely." [74]

In 1992, Congress enacted P.L. 102-356, § 16 of which required the FCC to promulgate regulations that prohibit broadcasting of indecent programming on radio and television from 6 a.m. to midnight, except for *public* radio and television stations that go off the air at or before midnight, which may broadcast such material beginning at 10 p.m. 47 U.S.C. § 303 note. In 1993, a three-judge panel of the U.S. Court of Appeals for the District of Columbia held the law unconstitutional, but, on June 30, 1995, the full court of appeals, by a 7-4 vote, overturned the panel and upheld the statute, except for its 10 p.m.-to-midnight ban imposed on non-public stations. [75]

The court of appeals found "that the Government has a compelling interest in supporting parental supervision of what children see and hear on the public airwaves," [76] and "that the Government has an independent and compelling interest in preventing minors from being exposed to indecent broadcasts." [77] The court found, in addition, that the statute used the least restrictive means to serve these interests. [78]

However, the court found that "Congress has failed to explain what, if any, relationship the disparate treatment accorded certain public stations bears to the compelling Government interest—or to any other legislative value—that Congress sought to advance when it enacted section 16(a)." [79] The court therefore held "that the section is unconstitutional insofar as it bars the broadcasting of indecent speech between the hours of 10:00 p.m. and midnight." [80]

Section 1465

This section makes it a crime knowingly to transport in interstate or foreign commerce for the purpose of sale or distribution, any "obscene, lewd, lascivious, or filthy" material, "or any other matter of indecent or immoral character." It also makes it a crime knowingly to travel in interstate commerce, or to use any facility or means of interstate commerce, for the purpose of transporting obscene material in interstate or foreign commerce. Section 1465 should be read as limited by the *Miller* standard. [81] The President's message that accompanied the original proposal that became P.L. 100-690 states:

> The term "facility of commerce" would include such things as the federal interstate highway system, federally numbered highways, and interstate railroads, even if such facility were used only intrastate. The term "means of interstate commerce" would include motor vehicles, boats, and airplanes capable of carrying goods in interstate commerce. The new offense would be committed, for example, by transporting obscene material by truck via Interstate 95 from Richmond to Alexandria, Virginia, with the intent that at least part of it would then be sold to customers outside of Virginia. [82]

In 1994, in Memphis, Tennessee, Robert and Carleen Thomas, a husband and wife from Milpitas, California, were convicted and sentenced to prison under 18 U.S.C. § 1465 for transmitting obscenity, from California, over interstate phone lines through their members-only computer bulletin board. The Sixth Circuit affirmed, holding that 18 U.S.C. § 1465 applies to computer transmissions. [83] The defendants had also raised a First Amendment issue, arguing that they "cannot select who gets the materials they make available on their bulletin boards. Therefore, they contend, BBS [bulletin board service] operators like Defendants will be forced to censor their materials so as not to run afoul of the standards of the community with the most restrictive standards." [84] The court did not decide the issue because it found that, in this case, the defendants had transmitted only to members whose addresses they knew, so "[i]f Defendants did not wish to subject themselves to liability in jurisdictions with less tolerant standards for determining obscenity, they could have refused to give passwords to members in those districts, thus precluding the risk of liability." [85]

In 1996, P.L. 104-104, § 507(b), amended 18 U.S.C. § 1465 to apply to any "interactive computer service."

Section 1466

This section makes it a crime for any person "engaged in the business of selling or transferring obscene matter" knowingly to receive or possess with intent to distribute any obscene material that has been transported in interstate or foreign commerce. Offering to sell or transfer, at one time, two or more copies of any obscene publication, or a combined total of five, shall create a rebuttable presumption that the person so offering them is "engaged in the business." In other words, if the government proved that the defendant had offered to sell, at one time, two or more copies of any obscene publication, or a combined total of five, then the defendant would be deemed to be "engaged in the business" unless he could prove otherwise.

Section 1466A

Section 504 of the PROTECT Act, P.L. 108-21 (2003), created this section, which makes it a crime knowingly to produce, distribute, receive, or possess, with or without intent to distribute, "a visual depiction of any kind, including a drawing, cartoon, sculpture, or painting," that depicts a minor engaging in sexually explicit conduct and is obscene or lacks serious literary, artistic, political, or scientific value. Section 1466A applies whether an actual minor is used or not, but covers only depictions of minors engaged in specified sexual activities, and not in lascivious exhibition of the genitals or pubic area. To the extent that § 1466A applies to non-obscene material produced without the use of an actual minor, it would be unconstitutional under *Ashcroft v. Free Speech Coalition*. [86]

Section 1467

This section provides for criminal forfeiture in obscenity cases. Specifically, it provides that a person convicted under the federal obscenity statute (18 U.S.C. §§ 1460-1469) shall forfeit to the United States (1) the obscene material, (2) property traceable to gross profits or other proceeds obtained from the obscene material, (3) property used or intended to be used to commit the offense, "if the court in its discretion so determines, taking into consideration the nature, scope, and proportionality of the use of the property in the offense." Thus, the court must determine, for example, whether a vehicle used to transport obscene material was owned by the defendant and was frequently used for that purpose, or, on the other hand, whether it had been borrowed from someone who had no knowledge of the use to which the defendant intended to put it.

The right of the United States to the property vests upon violation of the obscenity statute, not upon conviction. Therefore, property that was transferred between the violation and the conviction belongs to the United States, and shall also be forfeited. However, the statute contains an exception precluding forfeiture if the person to whom the property was transferred establishes that at the time of purchase he "was reasonably without cause to believe that the property was subject to forfeiture." Thus, if a person is convicted and the money he paid his lawyer to defend him can be traced to gross profits from the sale of obscene material, the lawyer may be required to forfeit the money unless he can convince the court that he had no reasonable cause to believe that the money was subject to forfeiture. [87] The Supreme Court has held that forfeiture of lawyers' fees under the federal drug forfeiture statute does not violate the Due Process Clause of the Fifth Amendment or criminal defendants' Sixth Amendment right to counsel of choice. [88]

Section 1467(c) provides that, prior to conviction, upon application of the United States, a court may issue an *ex parte* restraining order or injunction "to preserve the availability of property . . . for forfeiture." Section 1467(d) authorizes courts to issue warrants for the seizure of property solely upon a showing of "probable cause to believe that the property to be seized would, in the event of conviction, be subject to forfeiture and that an order under subsection (c) of this section may not be sufficient to assure the availability of the property for forfeiture." A federal district court declared these provisions unconstitutional insofar as they allow" seizure or restraint . . . without a prior adversarial hearing." [89] The court based this holding on the Supreme Court's decision in *Fort Wayne Books*, which is discussed in the section on RICO, below.

The court also declared two aspects of the post-conviction criminal forfeiture provisions unconstitutional. However, on appeal, the court of appeals, without addressing its merits, vacated the entire decision on the ground that, because the government had not threatened the plaintiffs with enforcement, the plaintiffs' claims were not ripe for judicial resolution. [90]

Section 1468

This section, enacted in 1988, makes it a crime "knowingly to utter[] obscene language or distribute[] any obscene matter by means of cable television or subscription services on television." Similarly, 47 U.S.C. § 559, enacted in 1984, makes it a crime to "transmit[] over any cable system any matter which is obscene or otherwise unprotected by the Constitution of the United States." The President's message that accompanied the original proposal that became section 1468 explained that the reason for its enactment was that ambiguities in Title 47 of the U.S. Code made it "unclear under what circumstances, if any, the federal government could enforce [47 U.S.C. § 559]." [91]

Section 1468 also provides that no provision of federal law is intended to preempt the power of the states, including their political subdivisions, "to regulate the uttering of language that is obscene or otherwise unprotected by the Constitution or the distribution of matter that is obscene or otherwise unprotected by the Constitution." There are also other statutes codified in title 47 of the U.S. Code that regulate obscenity and indecency on cable television; see below.

Section 1469

This section creates a rebuttable presumption that an item produced in one state and subsequently located in another, or produced outside the United States and subsequently located in the United States, was transported in interstate or foreign commerce. This means that, if the government proves the change of location, then, unless the defendant shows that the allegedly obscene material had not been transported in interstate or foreign commerce, it would be deemed to have been so transported.

Section 1470

This section, added by P.L. 105-314, § 401 (1998), makes it a crime to use the mail or interstate or foreign commerce knowingly to transfer obscene matter to a person under 16, knowing that such person is under 16.

D. Cable Television

In addition to 18 U.S.C. § 1468 and 47 U.S.C. § 559 (discussed above under "Section 1468"), both of which prohibit obscenity on cable television, various provisions in the Communications Act of 1934, codified in title 47 of the U.S. Code, regulate obscenity and indecency on cable television.

In 1994, in *Turner Broadcasting System v. Federal Communications Commission*, which did not involve obscenity or indecency, the Supreme Court held that cable television is entitled to full First Amendment protection. [92] It wrote in *Turner*: "In light of these fundamental technological differences between broadcast and cable transmission, application of the more relaxed standard of scrutiny, adopted in *Red Lion* and other broadcast cases is inapt when determining the First Amendment validity of cable regulation." [93] In 1996, in *Denver Area Educational Telecommunications Consortium, Inc. v. Federal Communications Commission*, a plurality of the Justices retreated from the Court's position in *Turner*. They wrote: "The Court's distinction in *Turner*, . . . between cable and broadcast television, relied on the inapplicability of the spectrum scarcity problem to cable. . . . While that distinction was relevant in *Turner* to the justification for structural regulations at issue there (the 'must carry' rules), it has little to do with a case that involves the effects of television viewing on children." [94]

In Part II of the *Denver Consortium* opinion, a plurality (four justices) upheld § 10(a) of the Cable Television Consumer Protection and Competition Act of 1992, 47 U.S.C. § 532(h), which permits cable operators to prohibit indecent material on leased access channels. [95] In upholding § 10(a), the Court, citing *Pacifica*, noted that cable television "is as 'accessible to children' as over-the-air broadcasting," has also "established a uniquely pervasive presence in the lives of all Americans," and can also "'confron[t] the citizen' in 'the privacy of the home,' . . . with little or no prior warning." [96] Applying something less than strict scrutiny, the Court concluded "that § 10(a) is a sufficiently tailored response to an extraordinarily important problem." [97]

It also found that "the statute is not impermissibly vague." [98]

In Part III of *Denver Consortium*, a majority (six justices) struck down § 10(b) of the 1992 Act, 47 U.S.C. § 532(j), which required cable operators, if they do not prohibit such programming on leased access channels, to segregate it on a single channel and block that channel unless the subscriber requests access to it in writing.

In this part of the opinion, the Court appeared to apply strict scrutiny, finding "that protection of children is a 'compelling interest,'" but "that, not only is [§ 10(b)] not a 'least restrictive alternative,' and is not 'narrowly tailored' to meet its legitimate objective, it also seems considerably 'more extensive than necessary.'" [99]

In Part IV, which only three justices joined, the Court struck down § 10(c), 42 U.S.C. § 531 note, which permitted cable operators to prohibit indecent material on public access channels. Without specifying the level of scrutiny they were applying, the justices concluded "that the Government cannot sustain its burden of showing that §10(c) is necessary to protect children or that it is appropriately tailored to secure that end." [100]

Another relevant statute concerning cable television is 47 U.S.C. § 544(d)(1), which provides that a franchising authority and a cable operator may specify, in granting or renewing a franchise, "that certain cable services shall not be provided or shall be provided subject to conditions, if such cable services are obscene or are otherwise unprotected by the Constitution of the United States." In addition, 47 U.S.C. § 544(d)(2)(A) provides: "In order to restrict the viewing of programming which is obscene or indecent, upon the request of a subscriber, a cable operator shall provide (by sale or lease) a device by which the subscriber can prohibit viewing of a particular cable service during a period selected by that subscriber." The Communications Decency Act of 1996, P.L. 104-104, which is known primarily for its provisions regulating computer-transmitted indecency, also contained provisions concerning cable television. Section 504 added § 640 to the Communications Act of 1934, 47 U.S.C. § 560, which provides:

> Upon request by a cable service subscriber, a cable operator shall, without charge, fully scramble or otherwise fully block the audio and video programming of each channel carrying such programming so that one not a subscriber does not receive it.

This section includes no restriction on the type of material that a subscriber may request to have blocked. Section 505 added § 641, 47 U.S.C. § 561, which provides:

> (a) In providing sexually explicit adult programming or other programming that is indecent on any channel of its service primarily dedicated to sexually-oriented programming, a multichannel video programming distributor shall fully scramble or otherwise fully block the video and audio portion of such channel so that one not a subscriber does not receive it.
> (b) Until a multichannel video programming distributor complies with the requirement set forth in subsection (a), the distributor shall limit the access of children to the programming referred to in that subsection by not providing such programming during the hours of the day (as determined by the [Federal Communications] Commission) when a significant number of children are likely to be viewing it.

On May 22, 2000, the Supreme Court declared § 505 unconstitutional, making clear, as it had not in *Denver Consortium*, that strict scrutiny applies to content-based speech restrictions on cable television. [101] The Court noted that "[t]he purpose of § 505 is to shield children from hearing or seeing images resulting from signal bleed," which refers to images or sounds that come through to non-subscribers, even though cable operators have "used scrambling in the regular course of business, so that only paying customers had access to certain programs." [102] Section 505 requires cable operators to implement more effective scrambling – to *fully* scramble or otherwise *fully* block programming so that non-subscribers do not receive it – or to "time channel," which, under an F.C.C. regulation meant to transmit the programming only from 10 p.m. to 6 a.m.

"To comply with the statute," the Court noted, "the majority of cable operators adopted the second, or 'time channeling,' approach. [103] The effect . . . was to eliminate altogether the transmission of the targeted programming outside the safe harbor period [6 a.m. to 10 p.m.] in affected cable service areas. In other words, for two-thirds of the day no household in those service areas could receive the programming, whether or not the household or the viewer wanted to do so." [104] The Court also noted that "[t]he speech in question was not thought by Congress to be so harmful that all channels were subject to restriction. Instead, the statutory disability applies only to channels 'primarily dedicated to sexually-oriented programming.'" [105]

As "a content-based speech restriction," the Court wrote, § 505 "can stand only if it satisfies strict scrutiny. . . . [I]t must . . . promote a compelling Government interest. . . . If a less restrictive alternative would serve the Government's purpose, the legislature must use that alternative." The Court did not explicitly say in this case that protecting children from sexually oriented signal bleed is a compelling interest, but assumed it, and addressed the question of whether § 505 constituted the least restrictive means to advance that interest. [106]

The Court noted that there is "a key difference between cable television and the Broadcasting media, which is the point on which this case turns: Cable systems have the capacity to block unwanted channels on a household-by-household basis. . . . [T]argeted blocking enables the Government to support parental authority without affecting the First Amendment interests of speakers and willing listeners . . . ." [107] Furthermore, targeted blocking is already required – by § 504 of the CDA, which, as noted above, requires cable operators, upon request by a cable service subscriber, to, without charge, fully scramble or otherwise fully block audio and video programming that the subscriber does not wish to receive. "When a plausible, less restrictive alternative is offered to a content-based speech restriction, it is the Government's obligation to prove that the alternative will be ineffective to achieve its goal. The Government has not met that burden here." [108] The Court concluded, therefore, that § 504, with adequate publicity to parents of their rights under it, constituted a less restrictive alternative to § 505.

One additional provision of the CDA affected cable television: § 506 amended 47 U.S.C. §§ 531(e) and 532(c)(2) to permit cable operators to refuse to transmit "obscenity, indecency, or nudity" on public access and leased access channels. [109]

E. The Communications Decency Act of 1996

The Communications Decency Act of 1996 (CDA) is Title V of the Telecommunications Act of 1996, P.L. 104-104. This report has previously noted amendments the Act made to 18 U.S.C. §§ 1462 and 1465, and provisions relating to cable television that it added to Title 47 of the U.S. Code. This section of the report examines § 502 of the Act, which would have limited indecent material transmitted by telecommunications devices and interactive computer services, and *Reno v. American Civil Liberties Union*, 521 U.S. 844 (1997), the Supreme Court decision holding it unconstitutional.

Section 502 rewrote 47 U.S.C. § 223(a) and added subsections (d) through (h) to 47 U.S.C. § 223. It did not amend subsections (b) or (c), which restrict commercial dial-a-porn services (see page 10, above). In *Reno*, the Supreme Court struck down § 223(a) in part and § 223(d) in whole.

47 U.S.C. § 223(a)

Prior to its amendment by § 603 of the PROTECT Act, P.L. 108-21 (2003), § 223(a)(1)(A) made it a crime, by means of a telecommunications device, knowingly to transmit a communication that is "obscene, lewd, lascivious, filthy, or indecent, with intent to annoy, abuse, threaten, or harass another person." Prior to its amendment by § 603 of the PROTECT Act, § 223(a)(1)(B)made it a crime, by means of a telecommunications device, knowingly to transmit a communication that is "obscene or indecent, knowing that the recipient of the communication is under 18 years of age. . . ." Section 223(a)(2) makes it a crime knowingly to permit any telecommunications facility under one's control to be used for any activity prohibited by § 223(a)(1) with the intent that it be used for such activity. [110]

Although the CDA defines "telecommunications," [111] it does not define "telecommunications device." However, it provides in § 223(h)(1)(B) that the term "does not include the use of an interactive computer service." [112] Thus, it appears that § 223(a)(1)(A) and (B) are intended to apply to communications, by telephone, fax machine, or computer, that are sent to particular individuals, not those that can be accessed by multiple users.

In *Reno v. American Civil Liberties Union*, the Supreme Court declared § 223(a)(1)(B) unconstitutional insofar as it applies to "indecent" communications.

Section 603 of the PROTECT Act amended § 223(a)(1)(A) by substituting "or child pornography" for "lewd, lascivious, filthy, or indecent." Thus, § 223(a)(1)(A) now bans only obscenity and child pornography, both of which are unprotected by the First Amendment. Section 223(a)(1)(A) thereby no longer raises the constitutional issue raised by the case cited in footnote 110.

Section 603 of the PROTECT Act amended § 223(a)(1)(A) by substituting "child pornography" for "indecent," so that it too now bans only obscenity and child pornography, and no longer raises the constitutional issue that gave rise to *Reno v. American Civil Liberties Union*.

47 U.S.C. § 223(d)

Prior to its amendment by § 603 of the PROTECT Act, § 223(d) made it a crime knowingly to use "an interactive computer service to send to a specific person or persons under 18 years of age, or . . . to display in a manner available to a person under 18 years of age, any . . . communication that, *in context, depicts or describes, in terms patently offensive as measured by contemporary community standards, sexual or excretory activities or organs* . . . ." (italics added) This prohibition seems equivalent to a prohibition of "indecent" material, but § 223(d) does not use the word "indecent," a fact of which the Supreme Court took note in *Reno* when it held § 223(d) unconstitutional. *See*, 521 U.S., at 871.

Section 603 of the PROTECT Act amended § 223(d)(1) by substituting "is obscene or child pornography" for the words italicized above. Section 223(d) thus no longer raises the constitutional issue that gave rise to *Reno v. American Civil Liberties Union*.

Reno v. American Civil Liberties Union

The Supreme Court found in this case that "the CDA is a content-based blanket restriction on speech . . . ." 521 U.S., at 868. As such, it may be found constitutional only if it serves "to promote a compelling interest" and is "the least restrictive means to further the articulated interest." [113] As for whether the CDA promotes a compelling interest, although the Court referred to "the legitimacy and importance of the congressional goal of protecting children from harmful materials" (521 U.S., at 849), it suggested that there may be less of a governmental interest in protecting older children from indecent material—at least such material as had artistic or educational value. *See*, 521 U.S., at 878.

As for whether the CDA is the least restrictive means to further the governmental interest, the Court found that "the Government [failed] to explain why a less restrictive provision would not be as effective as the CDA," 521 U.S., at 879. The CDA's "burden on adult speech," the Court held, "is unacceptable if less restrictive alternatives would be at least as effective in achieving the legitimate purpose that the statute was enacted to serve." *Id*. at 874. "[T]he Government may not 'reduc[e] the adult population . . . to . . . only what is fit for children.'" *Id*. at 875.

Could Congress reenact the CDA be reenacted in a narrower form that would be constitutional? The Supreme Court did not say, but it did not foreclose the possibility. It wrote:

> The arguments in this Court have referred to possible alternatives such as requiring that indecent material be "tagged" in a way that facilitates parental control of material coming into their homes, making exceptions for messages with artistic or educational value, providing some tolerance for parental choice, and regulating some portions of the Internet—such as commercial web sites— differently from others, such as chat rooms.

521 U.S., at 879.

F. Child Online Protection Act

On October 21, 1998, President Clinton signed into law the Omnibus Appropriations Act for fiscal year 1999 (P.L. 105-277), title XIV of which is the Child Online Protection Act (COPA). This law was an attempt to enact a constitutional version of the CDA. It differs from the CDA in two main respects: (1) it prohibits communication to minors only of material that is "harmful to minors," rather than material that is indecent, and (2) it applies only to communications for commercial purposes on publicly accessible Web sites. It defines "material that is harmful to minors" as pictures or words that —

> (A) the average person, applying contemporary community standards, would find, taking the material as a whole and with respect to minors, is designed to appeal to, or is designed to pander to, the prurient interest;
> (B) depicts, describes, or represents, in a manner patently offensive with respect to minors, an actual or simulated sexual act or sexual contact, an actual or simulated normal or perverted sexual act, or a lewd exhibition of the genitals or post-pubescent female breast; and
> (C) taken as a whole, lacks serious literary, artistic, political, or scientific value for minors. [114]

A communication is deemed to be for "commercial purposes" if it is made in the regular course of a trade or business with the objective of earning a profit; a communication need not propose a commercial transaction to be deemed to be for "commercial purposes." Requiring a viewer to use a credit card to gain access to material on the Internet would constitute a defense to prosecution.

In light of the Supreme Court's decision in *Reno*, is the Child Online Protection Act constitutional? The fact that COPA makes exceptions for messages with serious literary, artistic, political, or scientific value for minors, and that it applies only to commercial Web sites, makes it more likely than the CDA to be upheld. Nevertheless it may well, like the CDA, be found to "suppress[] a large amount of speech that adults have a constitutional right to receive and to address to one another." [115] This is because a Web site that is freely accessible, but is deemed "commercial" because it seeks to make a profit through advertisements, would apparently have to stop making its Web site freely accessible, or, in the alternative, would have to remove all words and pictures that might be deemed "harmful to minors" "by the standards of the community most likely to be offended by the message." [116]

COPA was scheduled to take effect on November 20, 1998, but a coalition of 17 civil liberties groups filed suit challenging it, and, on November 19, Judge Reed of the federal district court in Philadelphia, finding that there was a likelihood that the plaintiffs would prevail, issued a temporary restraining order against enforcement of the law. On February 1, 1999, he issued a preliminary injunction against enforcement pending a trial on the merits. [117] The preliminary injunction applies to all Internet users (not just the plaintiffs in this case) and provides that, even if the law is ultimately upheld, the Administration may not prosecute online speakers retroactively. On June 22, 2000, the U.S. Court of Appeals for the Third Circuit upheld the preliminary injunction, as it was "confident that the ACLU's attack on COPA's constitutionality is likely to succeed on the merits." [118] On May 13, 2002, the Supreme Court vacated the Third Circuit's opinion and remanded the case for further proceedings. It did not, however, remove the preliminary injunction against enforcement of the statute. Finally, on March 6, 2003, the Third Circuit again affirmed the district court's preliminary injunction. We now consider these four opinions in turn.

In issuing the preliminary injunction, the district court found that "[i]t is clear that Congress has a compelling interest in the protection of minors, including shielding them from materials that are not obscene by adult standards." [119] It also found, however, that "it is not apparent to this Court that the defendant can meet its burden to prove that COPA is the least restrictive means available to achieve the goal of restricting the access of minors to this material." [120] This is because "[t]he record before the Court reveals that blocking or filtering technology may be at least as successful as COPA would be in restricting minors' access to harmful material online without imposing the burden on constitutionally protected speech that COPA imposes on adult users or Web site operators." [121] In addition, "the sweeping category of forms of content that are prohibited — '*any communication*, picture, image, graphic image file, article, recording, writing, or *other matter of any kind*' (emphasis added [by the court])— could have been less restrictive of speech on the Web and more narrowly tailored to Congress' goal of shielding minors from pornographic teasers if the prohibited forms of content had included, for instances, only pictures, images, or graphic image files, which are typically employed by adult entertainment Web sites as 'teasers.' In addition, perhaps the goals of Congress could be served without the imposition of possibly excessive and serious criminal penalties, including imprisonment and hefty fines, for communicating speech that is protected as to adults or without exposing speakers to prosecution and placing the burden of establishing an affirmative defense on them instead of incorporating the substance of the affirmative defenses in the elements of the crime." [122]

On appeal, the Third Circuit affirmed on a different ground: "because the standard by which COPA gauges whether material is 'harmful to minors' is based on identifying 'contemporary community standards' the inability of Web publishers to restrict access to their Web sites based on the geographic locale of the site visitor, in and of itself, imposes an impermissible burden on constitutionally protected First Amendment speech." [123] This is because it results in communications available to a nationwide audience being judged by the standards of the community most likely to be offended. Applying strict scrutiny, the Third Circuit concluded that, though "[i]t is undisputed that the government has a compelling interest in protecting children from material that is harmful to them, even if not obscene by adult standards," [124] the government "may not regulate at all if it turns out that even the least restrictive means of regulation is still unreasonable when its limitations on freedom of speech are balanced against the benefits gained from those limitations." [125]

The Supreme Court held that COPA's "use of 'community standards' to identify 'material that is harmful to minors' . . . does not render the statute facially unconstitutional" – it "does not *by itself* render the statute substantially overbroad for purposes of the First Amendment." [126] Although there were five separate opinions in the case, eight of the nine justices favored remanding the case to the Third Circuit to consider whether the Act was nevertheless unconstitutional. Only Justice Stevens dissented, as only he believed that the use of community standards was a sufficient problem to warrant an affirmance of the Third Circuit's opinion.

The Court's statement that COPA's use of community standards does not *by itself* render the statute unconstitutional implies that COPA's use of community standards may nevertheless prove a factor among others that renders the statute unconstitutional. Justice Thomas, however, despite writing the opinion for the Court, including the *by itself* language quoted above, wrote, in a section of the opinion joined only by Chief Justice Rehnquist and Justice Scalia, "that any variance caused by the statute's reliance on community standards is not substantial enough to violate the First Amendment." [127] Justice Thomas also commented: "If a publisher wishes for its material to be judged only by the standards of particular communities [and not by the most puritanical community], then it need only take the simple step of utilizing a medium [a medium other than the Internet] that enables it to target the release of its materials into those communities." [128] Justice Stevens responded that the Court should "place the burden on parents to 'take the simple step of utilizing a medium that enables' . . . them to avoid this material before requiring the speaker to find another forum." [129]

Justice Kennedy, in a concurring opinion joined by Justices Souter and Ginsburg, found that "[w]e cannot know whether variation in community standards renders the Act substantially overbroad without first assessing the extent of speech covered and the variations in community standards with respect to that speech." [130]

Justice Kennedy believed that, before an assessment could be made, the Third Circuit should consider such questions as how much material COPA prohibits, how much the standard of the most puritanical community in the nation differ from standards of other communities, "what it means to evaluate Internet material 'as a whole,'" and the number of venues in which the government could prosecute violations of the Act. [131]

Justices O'Connor and Breyer wrote separate concurring opinions. Justice O'Connor agreed with Justice Kennedy that the plaintiffs had failed "to demonstrate substantial over breadth due solely to the variation between local communities," [132] and Justice Breyer, to avoid a First Amendment problem, would have construed the phrase "community standard" in the statute to mean a national standard.

On remand, the Third Circuit again affirmed the district court's preliminary injunction. It held "that the following provisions of COPA are not narrowly tailored to achieve the Government's compelling interest in protecting minors from harmful material and therefore fail the strict scrutiny test: (a) the definition of 'material that is harmful to minors,' . . . (b) the definition of 'commercial purposes,' . . . and (c) the '*affirmative defenses*' available to publishers, which require the technological screening of users for the purpose of age verification" (emphasis in original).

As for the definition of "material that is harmful to minors," the court found that the requirement that material be judged "as a whole" in determining whether it was designed to appeal to the prurient interests of minors and to lack serious value for minors meant "that each individual communication, picture, image, exhibit, etc. be deemed 'a whole' by itself . . . , rather than in context." Yet "one sexual image, which COPA may proscribe as harmful material, might not be deemed to appeal to the prurient interest of minors if it were to be viewed in the context of an entire collection of Renaissance artwork." The court also found the word "minor" in the definition of "material that is harmful to minors" to be "not narrowly drawn to achieve the statute's purpose," because it precludes Web publishers from knowing whether "an infant, a five-year old, or a person just shy of age seventeen . . . should be considered in determining whether the content of their Web site has 'serious . . . value for [those] minors'" or "will trigger the prurient interest, or be patently offensive with respect to those minors . . . ."

As for the definition of "commercial purposes," the court was "satisfied that COPA is not narrowly tailored to proscribe commercial pornographers and their ilk, as the Government contends, but instead prohibits a wide range of protected expression." As for the affirmative defense available to publishers, the court found that it "will likely deter many adults from accessing restricted content, because many Web users are simply unwilling to provide identification information in order to gain access to content . . . ."

The Third Circuit also found that voluntary "blocking and filtering techniques . . . may be substantially less restrictive than COPA in achieving COPA's objective of preventing a minor's access to harmful material." Finally, if held "that the plaintiffs will more probably prove at trial that COPA is substantially overbroad, and therefore, we will affirm the District Court on this independent ground as well."

G. Children's Internet Protection Act

The Children's Internet Protection Act (CIPA), P.L. 106-554 (2000), amended three federal statutes to provide that a school or library may not use funds it receives under these statutes to purchase computers used to access the Internet, or to pay the direct costs of accessing the Internet, and may not receive universal service discounts (other than for telecommunications services), unless the school or library enforces a policy "that includes the operation of a technology protection measure" that blocks or filters minors' Internet access to visual depictions that are obscene, child pornography, or "harmful to minors"; and that blocks or filters adults' Internet access to visual depictions that are obscene or child pornography. [133]

The sections of CIPA(1711 and 1712) that require schools and libraries to block or filter if they use federal funds for computers or for Internet access, provide that the blocking or filtering technology may be disabled "to enable access for bona fide research or other lawful purpose." The section of CIPA (1721) that requires schools and libraries to block or filter if they receive universal service discounts, provides that the blocking or filtering technology may be disabled "during use by an adult, to enable access for bona fide research or other lawful purpose." Sections 1711, 1712, and 1721 all contain identical definitions of "minor," "obscene," "child pornography," and "harmful to minors. They define a "minor" as a person under 17. They define "obscene" to have the meaning given such term in 18 U.S.C. § 1460, but that section does not define "obscene." [134] In the absence of a statutory definition, the courts will no doubt apply the *Miller* test to define the word.

Sections 1711, 1712, and 1721 all define "child pornography" to have the meaning given such term in 18 U.S.C. § 2256. That section defines "child pornography" as any "visual depiction" of "sexually explicit conduct" that is or appears to be of a minor, and defines "sexually explicit conduct" as various "actual or simulated" sexual acts or the "lascivious exhibition of the genitals or pubic area of any person." Child pornography need not be obscene under the *Miller* test; it is unprotected by the First Amendment even if it does not appeal to the prurient interest, is not patently offensive, and does not lack serious literary, artistic, scientific, or political value.

Sections 1711, 1712, and 1721 define "material that is harmful to minors" as any communication that –

(i) taken as a whole and with respect to minors, appeals to a prurient interest in nudity, sex, or excretion;
(ii) depicts, describes, or represents, in a patently offensive way with respect to what is suitable for minors, an actual or simulated sexual act or sexual contact, actual or simulated normal or perverted sexual acts, or a lewd exhibition of the genitals; and
(iii) taken as a whole, lacks serious literary, artistic, political, or scientific value as to minors. [135]

In *United States v. American Library Association*, a three-judge federal district unanimously declared CIPA unconstitutional and enjoined its enforcement insofar as it applies to libraries. [136] CIPA, like the CDA but unlike COPA, authorizes the government to appeal directly to the Supreme Court, and the government did so. On June 23, 2003, the Supreme Court reversed the district court, holding CIPA constitutional. [137]

The decision consisted of a four-justice plurality opinion by Chief Justice Rehnquist, concurring opinions by Justices Kennedy and Breyer, and dissenting opinions by Justices Stevens and Souter (the latter joined by Justice Ginsburg). The plurality noted that "Congress may not 'induce' the recipient [of federal funds] 'to engage in activities that would themselves be unconstitutional.'" The plurality therefore viewed the question before the Court as "whether [public] libraries would violate the First Amendment by employing the filtering software that CIPA requires." Does CIPA, in other words, effectively violate library *patrons* rights?

The plurality concluded that it does not. In so concluding, the plurality found that "Internet access in public libraries is neither a 'traditional' or a 'designated' public forum," [138] and that therefore it would not be appropriate to apply strict scrutiny to determine whether the filtering requirements are constitutional. [139] This means that the government did not have to demonstrate that CIPA serves a compelling interest (though Justice Kennedy in his concurrence noted that "all Members of the Court appear to agree" that it does) or that CIPA does so by the least restrictive means (the district court had found "that less restrictive alternatives to filtering software would suffice to meet Congress' goals").

The plurality acknowledged "the tendency of filtering software to 'overblock' – that is, to erroneously block access to constitutionally protected speech that falls outside the categories that software users intend to block." It found, however, that, "[a]ssuming that such erroneous blocking presents constitutional difficulties, any such concerns are dispelled by the ease with which patrons may have the filtering software disabled."

The plurality also considered whether CIPA imposes an unconstitutional condition on the receipt of federal assistance – in other words, does it violate public *libraries'* rights by requiring them to limit their freedom of speech if they accept federal funds? The plurality found that, assuming that government entities have First Amendment rights (it did not decide the question), CIPA does not infringe them.

This is because CIPA does not deny a benefit to libraries that do not agree to use filters; rather, the statute "simply insist[s] that public funds be spent for the purposes for which they were authorized." [140] "CIPA does not 'penalize' libraries that choose not to install such software, or deny them the right to provide their patrons with unfiltered Internet access. Rather, CIPA simply reflects Congress' decision not to subsidize their doing so."

In effect, then, the plurality seemed to view CIPA as raising no First Amendment issue other than the possible one of overblocking, which it found the statute to deal with adequately by its disabling provisions. Justice Kennedy, concurring, noted that, "[i]f some libraries do not have the capacity to unblock specific Web sites or to disable the filter or if it is shown that an adult user's election to view constitutionally protected Internet material is burdened in some other substantial way, that would be the subject for an as-applied challenge, not the facial challenge made in this case."

Justice Breyer would have applied "a form of heightened scrutiny," greater than rational basis scrutiny but "more flexible" than strict scrutiny, to assess CIPA's constitutionality. He would ask "whether the harm to speech-related interests is disproportionate in light of both the justifications and the potential alternatives." Applying this test, he concurred that CIPA is constitutional.

Justice Stevens found CIPA unconstitutional because of its "vast amount of 'overblocking,'" which he found not cured by the disabling provisions, because "[u]ntil a blocked site or group of sites is unblocked, a patron is unlikely to know what is being hidden and therefore whether there is any point in asking for the filter to be removed."

Justice Souter said that he would not "dissent if I agreed with the majority of my colleague . . . that an adult library patron could, consistently with the Act, obtain an unblocked terminal simply for the asking. . . . But the Federal Communications Commission, in its order implementing the Act, pointedly declined to set a federal policy on when unblocking by local libraries would be appropriate under the statute. . . . Moreover, the District Court expressly found that 'unblocking may take days, and may be unavailable, especially in branch libraries, which are often less well staffed than main libraries.'" Further, "the statute says only that a library 'may' unblock, not that it must." CRS-33

H. Misleading Domain Names on the Internet

This provision, 18 U.S.C. § 2252B, which was created by § 521 of the PROTECT Act, P.L. 108-21, was placed in the child pornography statute, but it concerns obscenity and "harmful to minors" material, and not child pornography, except to the extent that obscenity or "harmful to minors" material may also be child pornography. It makes it a crime knowingly to use a misleading domain name on the Internet with the intent to deceive a person into viewing material that is obscene, or with the intent to deceive a minor into viewing material that is "harmful to minors." It defines "harmful to minors" to parallel the *Miller* test for obscenity, as applied to minors.

I. RICO

The Federal Racketeer Influenced and Corrupt Organizations Act (RICO), was amended in 1984 to add the obscenity crimes specified in 18 U.S.C. §§ 1461-1465 to the definition of "racketeering activity" in 18 U.S.C. § 1961(1)(B). RICO makes it a crime for any person employed by or associated with any "enterprise" engaged in or affecting interstate or foreign commerce to participate in the affairs of the enterprise "through a pattern of racketeering activity." 18 U.S.C. § 1962(c). A "pattern of racketeering activity" means at least two acts of racketeering activity within ten years (excluding any period of imprisonment). 18 U.S.C. § 1961(5). Thus, if a person engages in two such activities, including the obscenity offenses specified, he is subject to prosecution under RICO in addition to, or instead of, prosecution for the particular activities.

RICO also provides for criminal forfeiture (18 U.S.C. § 1963), and its criminal forfeiture provision has been used in obscenity prosecutions; see *Alexander v.United States, infra*. In *FortWayne Books, Inc. v. Indiana*, 489 U.S. 46 (1989), the Supreme Court held that *pretrial* seizure, under the Indiana RICO statute, of books or other expressive materials, was unconstitutional. Although probable cause to believe that a person has committed a crime is sufficient to arrest him, "probable cause to believe that there are valid grounds for seizure is insufficient to interrupt the sale of presumptively protected books and films." *Id*. at 66. This presumption of First Amendment protection "is not rebutted until the claimed justification for seizing books or other publications is properly established in an adversary proceeding." *Id*. at 67. The Federal RICO statute, in any event, does not provide for pretrial seizure. [141]

In *Fort Wayne Books*, the Court did, however, uphold the constitutionality of including obscenity violations among the predicate offenses under a RICO statute. The Court rejected the argument "that the potential punishments available under the RICO law are so severe that the statute lacks a 'necessary sensitivity to first amendment rights.'" *Id*. at 57. Further, the Court held that such obscenity violations need not be "affirmed convictions on successive dates . . . in the same jurisdiction as that where the RICO charge is brought." *Id*. at 61.

The fact that the violations need not be affirmed convictions means that the obscenity violations may be proved as part of the RICO prosecution; no "warning shot" in the form of a prior conviction for obscenity is required. "As long as the standard of proof is the proper one with respect to all the elements of the RICO allegation – including proof, beyond a reasonable doubt, of the requisite number of constitutionally-proscribable predicate acts – all of the relevant constitutional requirements have been met." *Id*.

The fact that the predicate offenses need not be convictions in the same jurisdiction as that where the RICO charge is brought means that the predicate offenses can be violations which were based on community standards different from those of the jurisdiction where the RICO charge is brought. [142] "But, as long as, for example, each previous obscenity conviction was measured by the appropriate community's standard, we see no reason why the RICO prosecution – alleging a pattern of such violations – may take place only in a jurisdiction where two or more such offenses have occurred." *Id*. at 62. [143]

In *Alexander v. United States*, the Supreme Court addressed a question it had left open in *Fort Wayne Books*: whether there are First Amendment limitations to RICO forfeitures of assets that consist of expressive materials that are otherwise protected by the First Amendment. [144] The defendant in the case had been found guilty of selling four magazines and three videotapes that were obscene, and, on that basis, had been convicted under RICO. He was sentenced to six years in prison, fined $100,000, and ordered to pay the cost of prosecution, incarceration, and supervised release. He was also ordered to forfeit all his wholesale and retail businesses, including more than a dozen stores and theaters dealing in sexually explicit material, all the assets of these businesses (*i.e.*, expressive materials, whether or not obscene), and almost $9 million. The government chose to destroy, rather than sell, the expressive material.

The Supreme Court rejected the argument that the forfeiture of expressive materials constitutes prior restraint, as the forfeiture order "does not *forbid* petitioner from engaging in any expressive activities in the future, nor does it require him to obtain prior approval for any expressive activities." [145] Consequently, the Court analyzed the forfeiture "under normal First Amendment standards," and could see no reason why, "if incarceration for six years and a fine of $100,000 are permissible forms of punishment under the RICO statute, the challenged forfeiture of certain assets directly related to petitioner's racketeering activity is not. . . . [T]he First Amendment does not prohibit either stringent criminal sanctions for obscenity offenses or forfeiture of expressive materials as punishment for criminal conduct." [146]

The Court did, however, remand the case to the court of appeals to decide whether the forfeiture constituted an "excessive fine" under the Eighth Amendment. The same day, in another case, the Court held that the Excessive Fines Clause of the Eighth Amendment applies to forfeitures of property imposed by criminal statutes. [147]

J. Wiretaps

18 U.S.C. § 2516(1)(i) authorizes federal judges to approve "the interception of wire or oral communications" to collect evidence of violations of the federal obscenity statute (18 U.S.C. §§ 1460-1469). Section 201 of the PROTECT Act, P.L. 108-21 (2003), amended 18 U.S.C. § 2516(1)(c) to provide the same authorization with respect to child pornography crimes.

K. The Customs Service Provision

This statute, which is codified at 19 U.S.C. § 1305, prohibits importation of, among other things, obscene material, and provides, upon the appearance of any such material at a customs office, for its civil forfeiture. P.L. 100-690, § 7522(e), [148] amended 19 U.S.C. § 1305 to coordinate seizure by customs officers with criminal prosecutions under 18 U.S.C. § 1462. As the message of the President that accompanied the original proposal that became P.L. 100-690 explained,"While most obscene material seized by the Customs Service is forfeited under section 1305, some is of such a nature that it is referred for criminal prosecution as a violation of 18 U.S.C. 1462, importation of obscene material . . . ." [149] The amendment to section 1305 provides:

> [W]henever the Customs Service is of the opinion that criminal prosecution is appropriate or that further criminal investigation is warranted in connection with allegedly obscene material seized at the time of entry, the appropriate customs officer shall immediately transmit information concerning such seizure to the United States Attorney of the district of the *addressee's* residence. . . .

The amendment then sets forth the subsequent procedures to be followed by the U.S. Attorney.

ENDNOTES

[1] Despite its mentioning only "Congress," the First Amendment applies equally to all branches of the federal government and the states. Herbert v. Lando, 441 U.S. 153, 168 n.16 (1979).

[2] Child pornography is material that visually depicts sexual conduct by children. NewYork v. Ferber, 458 U.S. 747, 764 (1982). It is unprotected by the First Amendment even when it is not legally obscene; *i.e.,* child pornography need not meet the *Miller* test to be banned. For additional information,see CRS Report 95-406, *Child Pornography: Constitutional Principles and Federal Statutes.*

[3] In *Frisby v. Schultz*, 487 U.S. 474, 481 (1988), the Supreme Court noted: "The State may . . . enforce regulations of the time, place, and manner of expression which are content neutral [*i.e.,* "are *justified* without reference to the content of the speech," *Renton v. Playtime*

Theaters, Inc., 475 U.S. 41, 48 (1986) (emphasis in original)], are narrowly tailored to serve a significant [not necessarily a compelling] government interest, and leave open ample alternative channels of communication [but need not necessarily be the least restrictive means to further the government interest]."

[4] Sable Communications of California v. Federal Communications Commission, 492 U.S. 115, 126 (1989).

[5] Roth v. United States, 354 U.S. 476, 483 (1957). However, Justice Douglas, dissenting, wrote: "[T]here is no special historical evidence that literature dealing with sex was intended to be treated in a special manner by those who drafted the First Amendment." *Id.* at 514.

[6] *Id.* at 485.

[7] Miller v. California, 413 U.S. 15, 27 (1973).

[8] *Id.* at 24 (citation omitted). In *Brockett v. Spokane Arcades, Inc.*, 472 U.S. 491, 498 (1984), the Court struck down a state statute to the extent that it defined "prurient" as "that which incites lasciviousness or lust." The Court held that a publication was not obscene if it "provoked only normal, healthy sexual desires." To be obscene it must appeal to "a shameful or morbid interest in nudity, sex, or excretion." In *Manual Enterprises v.Day*, 370 U.S. 478, 480 (1962), the Court indicated that photographs of nude male models, although they appealed to the prurient interest and lacked literary, scientific, or other merit, were not patently offensive merely because they were aimed at homosexuals. In *Jenkins v. Georgia*, 418 U.S. 153, 160 (1974), the Court held that the film "Carnal Knowledge" was not obscene, writing: "Even though questions of appeal to the 'prurient interest' or of patent offensiveness are 'essentially questions of fact,' it would be a serious misreading of *Miller* to conclude that juries have unbridled discretion in determining what is 'patently offensive.'" In *Jacobellis v. Ohio*, 378 U.S. 184, 197 (1964), Justice Stewart, concurring, noted that "criminal laws in this area are constitutionally limited to hard-core pornography, which he would not attempt to define. Then followed his famous remark: "But I know it when I see it, and the motion picture involved in this case is not that." The motion picture was a French film called "Les Amants" ("The Lovers").

[9] 481 U.S. 497, 500 (1987). In *Hamling v. United States*, 418 U.S. 87, 105 (1974), the Court noted that a "community"was not any "precise geographic area," and suggested that it might be less than an entire state. In *Jenkins v. Georgia, supra* note 8, 418 U.S., at 157 (1974), the

Court approved a "trial court's instructions directing jurors to apply 'community standards' without specifying what 'community.'"

[10] Justice Scalia concurred in the result in *Pope v. Illinois*, but wrote: "[I]n my view it is quite impossible to come to an objective assessment of (at least) literary or artistic value, there being many accomplished people who have found literature in Dada, and art in the replication of a soup can. Since ratiocination has little to do with esthetics, the fabled 'reasonable man' is of little help in the inquiry, and would have to be replaced with, perhaps, the 'man of tolerably good taste' — a description that betrays the lack of an ascertainable standard. . . . I think we would be better advised to adopt as a legal maxim what has long been the wisdom of mankind: *De gustibus non est disputandum*. Just as there is no arguing about taste, there is no use litigating about it." *Id.* at 504-505.

[11] "When the validity of an act of the Congress is drawn in question, and even if a serious doubt of constitutionality is raised, it is a cardinal principle that this Court will first ascertain whether a construction of the statute is fairly possible by which the question may be avoided." Crowell v. Benson, 285 U.S. 22, 62 (1932).

[12] In *Federal Communications Commission v. Pacifica Foundation*, 438 U.S. 726, 749-750 (1978), the Supreme Court, upholding the power of the Federal Communications Commission to regulate a radio broadcast that was "indecent" but not obscene, wrote: We held in *Ginsberg v. New York*, 390 U.S. 629, that the government's interest in the "well-being of its youth" and in supporting "parents' claim to authority in their own household" justified the regulation of otherwise protected expression. *Id.,* at 640 and 639. The ease with which children may obtain access to broadcast material, coupled with the concerns recognized in *Ginsberg*, amply justify special treatment of indecent broadcasting. In *Reno v. American Civil Liberties Union*, 521 U.S. 844, 878 (1997), the Supreme Court suggested that the strength of the government's interest in protecting minors may vary depending upon the age of the minor, the parental control, and the artistic or educational value of the material in question.

[13] 492 U.S. 115, 126 (1989) (citations omitted). It might appear that regulations could be "narrowly drawn" or "carefully tailored" without being the "least restrictive means" to further a governmental interest. But *Sable*, on the same page, also uses the latter phrase (quoted above in the text accompanying note 4), and the Court has elsewhere made clear that the "narrow tailoring" required for content-based

restrictions is more stringent than that required for time, place, and manner restrictions (*see*, note 3, *supra*), where "least restrictive-alternative analysis is wholly out of place." Ward v. Rock Against Racism, 491 U.S. 781, 798-799 n.6 (1989).

[14] 394 U.S. 557, 565, 568 (1969). The Court has held that there is no right even to private possession of child pornography. Osborne v. Ohio, 495 U.S. 103 (1990).
[15] United States v. Reidel, 402 U.S. 351 (1971).
[16] United States v. 12 200-Ft. Reels of Film, 413 U.S. 123 (1973).
[17] *Id.* at 127. *See*, Edwards, *Obscenity in the Age of Direct Broadcast Satellite: A Final Burial for* Stanley v. Georgia*(?), a National Obscenity Standard, and Other Miscellany*, 33 William and Mary Law Review 949 (1992).
[18] 427 U.S. 50, 62 (1976).
[19] 475 U.S. 41, 43 (1986).
[20] *Young, supra* note 18, at 71-72 n.35.
[21] *Renton, supra* note 19, at 48 (emphasis in original).
[22] 427 U.S. at 71; 475 U.S. at 52.
[23] 422 U.S. 205 (1975).
[24] 452 U.S. 61 (1981).
[25] 493 U.S. 215 (1990).
[26] *Id.* at 220.
[27] *Id.* at 229.
[28] *Id.* at 236-237.
[29] *Id.* at 236.
[30] *Id.* at 237.
[31] 535 U.S. 425, 429 (2002).
[32] *Id.* at 430.
[33] *Id.*
[34] *Id.* at 438.
[35] *Id.* at 449.
[36] *Id.* at 460.
[37] 501 U.S. 560 (1991).
[38] 391 U.S. 367 (1968).
[39] *Barnes, supra* note 37, at 568.
[40] *Id.* at 582.
[41] *Id.* at 576 (emphasis in original).
[42] *Id.* at 590-591 (White, J., dissenting, joined by Justices Marshall, Blackmun, and Stevens).
[43] 529 U.S. 277 (2000).

[44] *Id.* at 292, 291.
[45] *Id.* at 310-311.
[46] *Id.* at 316.
[47] *Id.* at 294. The plurality said that, though nude dancing is "expressive conduct" [which ordinarily means it would be entitled to full First Amendment protection], "we think that it falls only within the outer ambit of the First Amendment's protection." *Id.* at 289. The opinion also quotes Justice Stevens to the same effect with regard to erotic materials generally. *Id.* at 294. In *United States v. Playboy Entertainment Group, Inc.*, *infra* note 100, 529 U.S., at 826, however, the Court wrote that it "cannot be influenced . . . by the perception that the regulation in question is not a major one because the speech is not very important."
[48] *Id.* at 301.
[49] *Id.* at 310.
[50] *Id.*
[51] *Id.* at 317-318.
[52] *Id.* at 324. Justice Stevens also wrote that the plurality was "mistaken in equating our secondary effects cases with the 'incidental burdens' doctrine applied in cases such as *O'Brien*. . . . The incidental burdens doctrine applies when speech and non-speech elements are combined in the same course of conduct"[internal quotation marks omitted], whereas secondary effects "are indirect consequences of protected speech." *Id.*
[53] *Barnes*, *supra* note 37, 501 U.S., at 585 n.2.
[54] Rowan v. Post Office Department, 397 U.S. 728, 738 (1970).
[55] Sable Communications of California, Inc. v. F.C.C., *supra* note 4, 492 U.S. 115 (1989).
[56] *Id.* at 126.
[57] *Id.* at 128.
[58] *Id.*
[59] *Id.* at 131.
[60] Section 223(b) provides that a person found guilty of knowingly communicating *obscene* dial-a-porn "shall be fined in accordance with title 18 of the United States Code, or imprisoned not more than two years, or both." Title 18, § 3571, provides for fines of up to $250,000 for individuals and up to $500,000 for organizations. A person found guilty of knowingly communicating *indecent* dial-a-porn "shall be fined not more than $50,000 or imprisoned not more

than six months, or both." Section 223(b) also provides for additional fines.

[61] Dial Information Services Corp. v. Thornburgh, 938 F.2d 1535 (2d Cir. 1991), *cert. denied*, 502 U.S. 1072 (1992).

[62] The court noted that the word has been "defined clearly" by the Federal Communications Commission, in the dial-a-porn context, "as the description or depiction of sexual or excretory activities or organs in a patently offensive manner as measured by contemporary community standards for the telephone medium." 938 F.2d, at 1540. The court noted that this definition tracks the one quoted in note 70, *infra. Id.* at 1541.

[63] *Id.* at 1541-1543; *see*, text accompanying note 4, *supra.*

[64] *See*, United States v. Merrill, 746 F.2d 458 (9th Cir. 1984), *cert. denied*, 469 U.S. 1165 (1985).

[65] United States v. 12 200-Ft. Reels of Film, 413 U.S. 123, 130 n.7 (1973).

[66] United States v. Keller, 259 F.2d 54, 57, 58 (3d Cir. 1958).

[67] This statute dates back to section 326 of the Communications Act of 1934, 48 Stat. 1091, which is why it uses only the term "radio." The term "radio," however, today includes broadcast television; *i.e.*, television transmitted over radio waves. In dictum, the Supreme Court noted that "the televising of nudes might well raise a serious question of programming contrary to 18 U.S.C. § 1464. . . ." F.C.C. v. Pacifica Foundation, 438 U.S. 726, 741 n.16 (1978); *see also, id.* at 750. "Radio communication" is defined for purposes of Title 47, U.S. Code, to mean "the transmission by radio of writing, signs, signals, *pictures*, and sounds of all kinds . . . ." 47 U.S.C. § 153(b) (emphasis added).

[68] 395 U.S. 367, 388 (1969). In this case, the Supreme Court upheld the constitutionality of the Federal Communication Commission's "fairness doctrine," which required broadcast media licensees to provide coverage of controversial issues of interest to the community and to provide a reasonable opportunity for the presentation of contrasting viewpoints on such issues.

[69] 438 U.S. 726 (1978).

[70] *Id.* at 729. The Court stated that, to be indecent, a broadcast need not have prurient appeal; "the normal definition of 'indecent' merely refers to nonconformance with accepted standards of morality." *Id.* at 740. The FCC holds that the concept "is intimately connected with the exposure of children to language that describes, in terms patently

offensive as measured by contemporary community standards for the broadcast medium, sexual or excretory activities and organs, at times of the day when there is a reasonable risk that children may be in the audience." *Id.* at 732. *See*, note 62, *supra*.

[71] *Id.* at 748-749.
[72] *Id.* at 750.
[73] *Id.* at 733 (quoting the FCC).
[74] Action for Children's Television v. Federal Communications Commission (ACT II), 932 F.2d 1504, 1509 (D.C. Cir. 1991), *cert. denied*, 503 U.S. 913 (1992).
[75] Action for Children's Television v. Federal Communications Commission (ACT III), 58 F.3d 654 (D.C. Cir. 1995) (en banc), *cert. denied*, 516 U.S. 1043 (1996).
[76] *Id.* at 661.
[77] *Id.* at 663.
[78] The court wrote: "While we apply strict scrutiny to regulations of this kind regardless of the medium affected by them, our assessment of whether section 16(a) survives that scrutiny must necessarily take into account the unique context of the broadcast media." *Id.* at 660. Chief Judge Edwards, in his dissent, wrote: "This is the heart of the case, plain and simple," as "[t]he majority appears to recognize that section 16(a) could not withstand constitutional scrutiny if applied against *cable* television operators." *Id.* at 671.
[79] *Id.* at 668.
[80] *Id.* at 669. Note that the court struck down the 10 p.m.-to-midnight ban not because it failed strict scrutiny under the First Amendment, but because it applied only to non-public stations. Chief Judge Edwards, in his dissent, commented that "the majority appears to invite Congress to extend the 6 a.m. to midnight ban to all broadcasters, without exception." *Id.* at 670 n.1.
[81] United States v. Alexander, 498 F.2d 934, 935-936 (2d Cir. 1974).
[82] H.R. Doc. No. 100-129, 100th Cong., 1st Sess. 78 (1987).
[83] United States v. Thomas, 74 F.3d 701 (6th Cir. 1996), *cert. denied*, 519 U.S. 820 (1996). The court cited another conviction under 18 U.S.C. § 1465 for computer pornography — this one by an Air Force court. United States v. Maxwell, 42 M.J. 568 (A.F.Ct.Crim. App. 1995).
[84] *Id.* at 711. In *Reno v. American Civil Liberties Union*, *supra* note 12, the Supreme Court noted that "the 'community standards' criterion as applied to the Internet means that any communication available to a

[ ]   nation-wide audience will be judged by the standards of the community most likely to be offended by the message." In *Ashcroft v. American Civil Liberties Union, infra* note 116, the Supreme Court held that the use of community standards to assess "harmful to minors" material on the Internet is not by itself unconstitutional.
[85] *Id.*
[86] 535 U.S. 434 (2002).
[87] The lawyer could argue that the money came from a source independent of his client's alleged criminal activity; it seems less certain whether he could argue that, at the time his client paid him, he (the lawyer) was reasonably without cause to believe that the money was subject to forfeiture because he reasonably believed that his client would be found not guilty.
[88] Caplin & Drysdale v. United States, 491 U.S. 617 (1989).
[89] American Library Association v. Thornburgh, 713 F. Supp. 469, 485 (D.D.C. 1989), *vacated sub nom.* American Library Association v. Barr, 956 F.2d 1178 (D.C. Cir. 1992).
[90] *Id.* at 1196.
[91] H.R. Doc. No. 100-129, *supra* note 82, at 93.
[92] 512 U.S. 622 (1994).
[93] *Id.* at 639.
[94] 518 U.S. 727, 748 (1996).
[95] The Cable Communications Policy Act of 1984, P.L. 98-549, had required cable operators to provide leased access and public access channels free of operator editorial control. 47 U.S.C. §§ 531(e), 532(c)(2). These two provisions were amended in 1996 by § 506 of the Communications Decency Act to permit cable operators to refuse to transmit "obscenity, indecency, or nudity."
[96] *Denver Consortium, supra* note 94, 518 U.S., at 744-745.
[97] *Id.* at 743.
[98] *Id.* at 753.
[99] *Id.* at 755.
[100] *Id.* at 766. Two other justices concurred in the judgment that § 10(c) is invalid, but for different reasons.
[101] United States v. Playboy Entertainment Group, Inc., 529 U.S. 803, 813 (2000). The decision was 5-4, with Justices Breyer, Rehnquist, O'Connor, and Scalia dissenting.
[102] *Id.* at 806.
[103] *Id.* They may have done so because fully blocking or fully scrambling "appears not be economical" (*id.* at 808) or because the technology is

imperfect and cable operators attempting to fully block or fully scramble might have still been "faced with the possibility of sanctions for intermittent bleeding" (*id.* at 821).

[104] *Id.* at 806-807.

[105] *Id.* at 812.

[106] The Court wrote: "Even upon the assumption that the Government has an interest in substituting itself for informed and empowered parents, its interest is not sufficiently compelling to justify this widespread restriction on speech." *Id.* at 825. The Court, in other words, while assuming that the government has a compelling interest in aiding parents in protecting their children from sexually oriented signal bleed, did not find that the government has a compelling interest in protecting children from such material when their parents allow it into the home. The Court also noted "the possibility that a graphic image could have a negative impact on a young child." *Id.* at 826. This suggests the possibility that the Court might not find a compelling interest in shielding older children from sexually oriented material.

[107] *Id.* at 815.

[108] *Id.* at 816.

[109] Justice Kennedy, in the only footnote to his concurring and dissenting opinion in *Denver Consortium*, wrote that the constitutionality of the amendments made by § 506, "to the extent they differ from the provisions here [§§ 10(a) and 10(c) of the 1992 Act], is not before us." 518 U.S., at 782.

[110] In *Apollo Media Corp. v. Reno*, 19 F. Supp.2d 1081, 1084 (N.D. Cal. 1998), *aff'd*, 526 U.S. 1061 (1999), the plaintiff sought to enjoin enforcement of § 223(a)(1)(A) and § 223(a)(2) "on the grounds that . . . , to the extent that they prohibit 'indecent' communications made 'with an intent to annoy,' [they] are impermissibly overbroad and vague. . . ." The three-judge court denied the plaintiff's request because it found that "the provisions regulate only 'obscene' communications." The Supreme Court affirmed without a written opinion. The plaintiffs reportedly had appealed because they believed that the fact that the word "indecent" was in the statute could have a chilling effect on indecent nonobscene expression, even if the law was not enforceable against such expression.

[111] Section 3 of P.L. 104-104 added to 47 U.S.C. § 153 the following definition of "telecommunications": "the transmission, between or among points specified by the user, of information of the user's

choosing, without change in the format or content of the information as sent and received." The conference report adds that this information includes "voice, data, image, graphics, and video."

[112] Section 230(f)(2) (added by § 509) defines "interactive computer service" as "any information service, system, or access software provider that provides or enables computer access by multiple users to a computer server, including specifically a service or system that provides access to the Internet and such systems operated or services offered by libraries or educational institutions."

[113] *Sable, supra* note 4.

[114] Despite the fact that only the first prong of this test refers to "community standards," community standards are apparently also intended to be used in applying the second prong. See footnote 7 of the Supreme Court's opinion, *infra* note 117.

[115] *Reno, supra* note 12, 521 U.S., at 874.

[116] *Id.* at 877-878. In support of the law's constitutionality, one might analogize its restriction on speech to state law bans on "public display and unattended sale, in places where minors might be present, of 'obscene-as-to-minors' materials." *See*, Eugene Volokh, *Freedom of Speech, Shielding Children, and Transcending Balance*, 1997 SUP. CT. REV. 141, 186.

[117] American Civil Liberties Union v. Reno, 31 F. Supp.2d 473 (E.D. Pa. 1999), *aff'd*, 217 F.3d 162 (3d Cir. 2000), *vacated and remanded sub nom.* Ashcroft v. American Civil Liberties Union, 535 U.S. 564 (2002), *aff'd on remand*, 322 F.3d 240 (3d Cir. 2003).

[118] *Id.*, 217 F.3d, at 166.

[119] *Id.*, 31 F. Supp.2d, at 495.

[120] *Id.* at 497.

[121] *Id.*

[122] *Id.*

[123] *Id.*, 217 F.3d, at 166.

[124] *Id.* at 173.

[125] *Id.* at 179.

[126] *Ashcroft, supra* note 117, 535 U.S. 564, 585 (2002) (emphasis in original).

[127] *Id.*

[128] *Id.* at 583.

[129] *Id.* at 606 n.2.

[130] *Id.* at 597.

[131] *Id.* at 600.

[132] *Id.* at 589.
[133] Section 1711 amends Title III of the Elementary and Secondary Education Act of 1965, 20 U.S.C. §§ 6801 *et seq.* Section 1712 amends section 224 of the Museum and Library Services Act, 20 U.S.C. § 9134, which is part of the Library Services and Technology Act (LSTA), which is Title II of the Museum and Library Services Act. Section 1721 amends section 254(h) of the Communications Act of 1934, 47 U.S.C. § 254(h), which establishes the "universal service discount," or "E-rate," for schools and libraries. Only sections 1712 and 1721 (insofar as it applies to libraries) were at issue in the case before the three-judge district court and the Supreme Court.
[134] Nor does any other section of the U.S. Code, except 20 U.S.C. § 952(*l*), which defines it for purposes of grants by the National Endowment for the Arts, and does so in a manner that parallels the *Miller* test, except that it does not apply community standards to the determination of whether material is patently offensive.
[135] This three-part test is similar to that of the Child Online Protection Act, 47 U.S.C. § 231(e), but three differences are that CIPA applies only to images, whereas COPA applies to images and words; CIPA does not, like COPA, provide that the prurience determination be made in accordance with the views of "the average person applying contemporary community standards"; and CIPA does not, like COPA, allow an image or description of the "post-pubescent female breast" to be found harmful to minors.
[136] 201 F. Supp.2d 401 (E.D. Pa. 2002). The district court struck down § 1712(a)(2), which concerns LSTA funds, and § 1721(b) which concerns E-rate discounts for libraries. The provisions affecting schools were not challenged.
[137] No. 02-316 (U.S., June 23, 2003).
[138] The district court had found "that when the government provides Internet access in a public library, it has created a designated public forum," and that "content-based restrictions on speech in a designated public forum are most clearly subject to strict scrutiny when the government opens a forum for virtually unrestricted use by the general public for speech on a virtually unrestricted range of topics, while selectively excluding particular speech whose content it disfavors." 201 F.Supp.2d 401, 457, 460 (E.D. Pa. 2002).
[139] The reason the plurality found that Internet access in public libraries is not a public forum is that "[a] public library does not acquire Internet terminals in order to create a public forum for Web

publishers to express themselves, any more than it collects books in order to provide a public forum for authors of books to speak. It provides Internet access, not to 'encourage a diversity of views from private speakers,' but for the same reasons it offers other library resources: to facilitate research, learning, and recreational pursuits by furnishing materials of requisite and appropriate quality."

[140] For additional information on the question of unconstitutional conditions, see CRS Report 95-815, *Freedom of Speech and Press: Exceptions to the First Amendment.*

[141] *See,* Fort Wayne Books, Inc. v. Indiana, 489 U.S., at 67 n.13.

[142] This could be the case even in a RICO prosecution based on predicate offenses in a different part of the same state, as the relevant community may be an area less than the entire state. *See,* Hamling v. United States, 418 U.S. 87, 105 (1974).

[143] Although the Court uses the word "conviction" in this sentence, there appears to be no reason why a RICO prosecution could not be based on a violation in another jurisdiction that had not previously been prosecuted in that jurisdiction. In such a case, the prosecution would have to prove beyond a reasonable doubt that the laws (including, in an obscenity case, the community standards) of the state where the predicate offense occurred had been violated.

[144] 509 U.S. 544 (1993).

[145] *Id.* at 550-551.

[146] *Id.* at 554-555.

[147] Austin v. United States, 509 U.S. 602 (1993).

[148] Subsection (e) apparently should have been "(d)," as there is no "(d)" following "(c)."

[149] H.R. Doc. 100-129, *supra* note 82, at 82.

Chapter 4

OBSCENITY, CHILD PORNOGRAPHY, AND INDECENCY: RECENT DEVELOPMENTS AND PENDING ISSUES[*]

Henry Cohen

PREFACE

The First Amendment provides that "Congress shall make no law... abridging the freedom of speech, or of the press...." The First Amendment applies, with two exceptions, to pornography and indecency, with those terms being used to refer to any words or pictures of a sexual nature. The two exceptions are obscenity and child pornography; because these are not protected by the First Amendment, they may be, and have been, made illegal. Pornography and indecency that are protected by the First Amendment may nevertheless be restricted in order to limit minors' access to them.

OBSCENITY [1]

To be legally obscene, and therefore unprotected by the First Amendment, pornography must, at a minimum, "depict or describe patently

---

[*] Excerpted from CRS Report 98-670 A dated June 24, 2003

offensive 'hard core' sexual conduct."[2] The Supreme Court has created a three-part test, known as the *Miller* test, to determine whether a work is obscene. The *Miller* test asks:

> (a) whether the "average person applying contemporary community standards" would find that the work, taken as a whole, appeals to the prurient interest; (b) whether the work depicts or describes, in a patently offensive way, sexual conduct specifically defined by the applicable state law; and (c) whether the work, taken as a whole, lacks serious literary, artistic, political, or scientific value. [3]

In *Pope v. Illinois*, the Supreme Court clarified that "the first and second prongs of the *Miller* test—appeal to prurient interest and patent offensiveness—are issues of fact for the jury to determine applying contemporary community standards." However, as for the third prong, "[t]he proper inquiry is not whether an ordinary member of any given community would find serious literary, artistic, political, or scientific value in allegedly obscene material, but whether a reasonable person would find such value in the material, taken as a whole."[4]

Obscenity: Recent Developments

The Communications Decency Act of 1996 (P.L. 104-104, § 507) expanded the law prohibiting the importation of, or interstate commerce in, obscenity (18 U.S.C. §§ 1462, 1465) to apply to the use of an "interactive computer service" for that purpose. It defined "interactive computer service" to include "a service or system that provides access to the Internet." 47 U.S.C. § 230(e)(2). These provisions were not affected by the Supreme Court's decision in *Reno v. American Civil Liberties Union* declaring unconstitutional two provisions of the CDA that would have restricted indecency on the Internet.[5]

Obscenity: Pending Issues

In *Reno*, the Court noted, in dictum, that "the 'community standards' criterion as applied to the Internet means that any communication available to a nationwide audience will be judged by the standards of the community most likely to be offended by the message."[6] This suggested that, at least with respect to obscenity on the Internet, the Court might replace the community standards criterion, except perhaps in the case of Internet services where the defendant makes a communication available only to subscribers and can thereby restrict the communities in which he makes a posting accessible. However, in *Ashcroft v. American Civil Liberties Union*, decided May 13, 2002, the Court held that the use of community standards does not by itself render a statute banning "harmful to minors" material on the Internet unconstitutional. (See below under "Indecency.")

CHILD PORNOGRAPHY [7]

Child pornography is material "that *visually* depict[s] sexual conduct by children below a specified age."[8] It is unprotected by the First Amendment even when it is not obscene; *i.e.*, child pornography need not meet the *Miller* test to be banned.[9] The reason that child pornography is unprotected is that it "is intrinsically related to the sexual abuse of children . . . . Indeed, there is no serious contention that the legislature was unjustified in believing that it is difficult, if not impossible, to halt the exploitation of children by pursuing only those who produce the photographs and movies."[10]

Federal law bans interstate commerce (including by computer) in child pornography (18 U.S.C. §§ 2252, 2252A), defines "child pornography" as "any visual depiction" of "sexually explicit conduct" involving a minor, and defines "sexually explicit conduct" to include not only various sex acts but also the "lascivious exhibition of the genitals or pubic area of any person." 18 U.S.C. § 2256.

Child Pornography: Recent Developments

In 1994, Congress amended the child pornography statute to provide that "lascivious exhibition of the genitals or pubic area of any person" "is not limited to nude exhibitions or exhibitions in which the outlines of those areas were discernible through clothing." 18 U.S.C. § 2252 note. This amendment expressed Congress's support for a court decision upholding a conviction for possessing "videotapes that focus on the genitalia and pubic area of minor females . . . even though these body parts are covered by [opaque] clothing."[11] Then, the Child Pornography Prevention Act of 1996 (CPPA) created a definition of "child pornography" that included visual depictions that *appear* to be of a minor, even if no minor was actually used. 18 U.S.C. §

2256(8). The statute, thus, may be read to include visual depictions using adult actors who appear to be minors, as well as computer graphics and drawings or paintings done without any models.

On April 16, 2002, in *Ashcroft v. Free Speech Coalition*, the Supreme Court declared the CPPA unconstitutional to the extent that it prohibited pictures that were not produced with actual minors.[12] Child pornography, to be unprotected by the First Amendment, must either be obscene or depict actual children engaged in sexual activity (including "lascivious" poses), or actual children whose images have been "morphed" to make it appear that the children are engaged in sexual activity. The Court observed in *Ashcroft* that statutes that prohibit child pornography that use real children are constitutional because they target "[t]he production of the work, not the content." The CPPA, by contrast, targeted the content, not the means of production. The government's rationales for the CPPA included that "[p]edophiles might use the materials to encourage children to participate in sexual activity" and might "whet their own sexual appetites" with it, "thereby increasing . . . the sexual abuse and exploitation of actual children." The Court found these rationales inadequate because the government "cannot constitutionally premise legislation on the desirability of controlling a person's private thoughts" and "may not prohibit speech because it increases the chance an unlawful act will be committed 'at some indefinite future time.'"

The government also argued that the existence of "virtual" child pornography "can make it harder to prosecute pornographers who do use real minors," because, "[a]s imaging technology improves . . . , it becomes more difficult to prove that a particular picture was produced using actual children." This rationale, the Court found, "turns the First Amendment upside down. The Government may not suppress lawful speech as a means to suppress unlawful speech."

In response to *Ashcroft*, Congress enacted TitleV of the Prosecutorial Remedies and Other Tools to end the Exploitation of Children Today Act of 2003, or PROTECT Act, Public Law 108-21. This statute prohibits any "digital image, computer image, or computer-generated image that is, or is indistinguishable from, that of a minor engaging in sexually explicit conduct. It also prohibits "a visual depiction of any kind, including a drawing, cartoon, sculpture, or painting, that . . . depicts a minor engaging in sexually explicit conduct," and is obscene or lacks serious literary, artistic, political, or scientific value. Section 603 of the PROTECT Act amended the CDA to apply to child pornography transmitted via the Internet.

Child Pornography: Pending Issues

To the extent that the PROTECT Act prohibits non-obscene child pornography that was produced without the use of an actual child, it may be challenged as unconstitutional.

INDECENCY [13]

"Indecency" has no precise definition. The Supreme Court has said that "the normal definition of 'indecent' merely refers to nonconformance with accepted standards of morality."[14] More specifically, the term has been defined as material that "depicts or describes, in terms patently offensive as measured by contemporary community standards, sexual or excretory activities or organs."[15]

Indecent material is protected by the First Amendment unless it constitutes obscenity or child pornography. Indecent material that is protected by the First Amendment may be restricted by the government only "to promote a compelling interest" and only by "the least restrictive means to further the articulated interest."[16] The Supreme Court has "recognized that there is a compelling interest in protecting the physical and psychological well-being of minors. This interest extends to shielding minors from the influence of literature that is not obscene by adult standards."[17]

There are federal statutes in effect that limit, but do not ban, indecent material transmitted via telephone, broadcast media, and cable television.[18] There are also many state statutes that ban the distribution to minors of material that is "harmful to minors." Material that is "harmful to minors" under these statutes tends to be defined more narrowly than material that is "indecent," in that material that is "harmful to minors" is generally limited to material of a sexual nature that has no serious value for minors. The Supreme Court has upheld New York's "harmful to minors" statute.[19]

Indecency: Recent Developments

In 1997, the Supreme Court declared unconstitutional two provisions of the Communications Decency Act of 1996 that would have prohibited indecent communications, by telephone, fax, or e-mail, to minors, and would have prohibited use of an "interactive computer service" to display indecent material "in a manner available to a person under 18 years of age."[20] This latter prohibition would have banned indecency from public (*i.e.*, non-subscription)Web sites.

The CDA was succeeded by the Child Online Protection Act (P.L. 105-277), which differs from the CDA in two main respects: (1) it prohibits communication to minors only of "material that is harmful to minors," rather than material that is indecent, and (2) it applies only to communications for commercial purposes on publicly accessible Web sites. "Material that is harmful to minors" is defined as material that (A) is prurient, as determined by community standards, (B) "depicts, describes, or represents, in a manner patently offensive with respect to minors," sexual acts or a lewd exhibition of the genitals or post-pubescent female breast, and (C) "lacks serious literary, artistic, political, or scientific value for minors." A communication is deemed to be for "commercial purposes" if it is made in the regular course of a trade or business with the objective of earning a profit. Requiring a viewer to use a credit card to gain access to the material would constitute a defense to prosecution. The law was scheduled to take effect on November 20, 1998, but a suit challenging it was filed, and a federal district court in Philadelphia, finding that there was a likelihood that the plaintiffs would prevail, issued a preliminary injunction against enforcement of the statute pending a trial on the merits.[21] The Third Circuit upheld the preliminary injunction, and, on May 13, 2002, the Supreme Court vacated and remanded the Third Circuit's decision, but did not remove the preliminary injunction. On March 6, 2003, the Third Circuit again affirmed the district court's preliminary injunction.

Indecency: Pending Issues

In light of the Supreme Court's decision in *Reno*, is the Child Online Protection Act constitutional? The primary problem the Court found with the CDA was that, "[i]n order to deny minors access to potentially harmful speech, the CDA effectively suppresses a large amount of speech that adults have a constitutional right to receive and to address to one another."[22] The fact that COPA does not apply to material with serious literary, artistic, political, or scientific value for minors, and that it applies only to commercial Web sites, makes it more likely than the CDA to be upheld. Nevertheless it may well, like the CDA, be found to "suppress[] a large amount of speech that adults have a constitutional right to receive and to address to one another." This is because a Web site that is freely accessible, but is deemed "commercial" because it seeks to make a profit through advertisements, would apparently have to stop making its Web site freely accessible, or, in the alternative, would have to remove all words and pictures that might be deemed "harmful to minors" according to the standards of the community most likely to be offended by the material. In its May 13, 2002 decision, the Supreme Court held that COPA's use of community standards does not by itself render the statute unconstitutional, but it remanded the case to the Third Circuit to consider whether it is unconstitutional nonetheless, and the Third Circuit held that it is.

THE CHILDREN'S INTERNET PROTECTION ACT (CIPA), P.L. 106-554 [23]

CIPA restricts access to obscenity, child pornography, and material that is "harmful to minors," and so is discussed here separately. CIPA amended three federal statutes to provide that a school or library may not use funds it receives under these statutes to purchase computers used to access the Internet, or to pay the direct costs of accessing the Internet, and may not receive universal service discounts, unless the school or library enforces a policy to block or filter minors' Internet access to visual depictions that are obscene, child pornography, or harmful to minors; and enforces a policy to block or filter adults' Internet access to visual depictions that are obscene or child pornography. It provides, however, that filters may be disabled "for bona fide research or other lawful purposes."

On May 31, 2002, a three-judge federal district court declared CIPA unconstitutional and enjoined its enforcement insofar as it applies to libraries. (The provisions affecting schools were not challenged.) The government appealed directly to the Supreme Court, which, on June 23, 2003, reversed the district court, holding CIPA constitutional.[24] The plurality opinion acknowledged "the tendency of filtering software to 'overblock' – that is, to erroneously block access to constitutionally protected speech that falls outside the categories that software users intend to block." It found, however, that, "[a]ssuming that such erroneous blocking presents constitutional difficulties, any such concerns are dispelled by the ease with which patrons may have the filtering software disabled." The plurality also found that CIPA does not deny a benefit to libraries that do not agree to use filters; rather, the statute "simply insist[s] that public funds be spent for the purposes for which they were authorized."

ENDNOTES

[1] For additional information, see CRS Report 95-804, *Obscenity and Indecency: Constitutional Principles and Federal Statutes.*
[2] Miller v. California, 413 U.S. 15, 27 (1973).
[3] *Id.* at 24 (citation omitted).
[4] 481 U.S. 497, 500 (1987).
[5] 521 U.S. 844 (1997).
[6] *Id.* at 877-878.
[7] For additional information, see CRS Report 95-406, *Child Pornography: Constitutional Principles and Federal Statutes.*
[8] New York v. Ferber, 458 U.S. 747, 764 (1982) (italics in original).
[9] This means that child pornography may be banned even if does not appeal to the prurient interest, is not patently offensive, and does not lack literary, artistic, political, or scientific value. See Ferber, *supra* note 8, 458 U.S., at 764.
[10] *Ferber, supra* note 8, 458 U.S., at 759-760.
[11] United States v. Knox, 977 F.2d 815, 817 (3d Cir. 1992), *vacated and remanded,* 510 U.S. 375 (1993); 32 F.3d 733 (3d Cir. 1994), *cert. denied,* 513 U.S. 1109 (1995).
[12] 535 U.S. 234 (2002).
[13] For additional information, see CRS Report 95-804, *Obscenity and Indecency: Constitutional Principles and Federal Statutes.*
[14] Federal Communications Commission v. Pacifica Foundation, 438 U.S. 726, 740 (1978).
[15] This quotation is from 47U.S.C. § 223(d), a provision of the CDA that the Supreme Court held unconstitutional. This definition is similar to the FCC's definition of "indecent" in the context of dial-a-porn and broadcast media. *See,* Dial Information Services Corp. v. Thornburgh, 938 F.2d 1535, 1540 (2d Cir. 1991), *cert. denied,* 502 U.S. 1072 (1992); *Pacifica, supra* note 14, 438 U.S., at 732.
[16] Sable Communications of California v. Federal Communications Commission, 492 U.S. 115, 126 (1989).
[17] *Id.*
[18] 47 U.S.C. § 223(b) (commercial dial-a-porn), 18 U.S.C. § 1464, 47 U.S.C. § 303 note (broadcast media), 47 U.S.C. §§ 531(e), 532(c)(2), 532(h), 559-561 (cable television). The Supreme Court declared section 561 unconstitutional. United States v. Playboy Entertainment Group, Inc. v. United States, 529 U.S. 803 (2000).
[19] Ginsberg v. New York, 390 U.S. 629 (1968).

[20] Reno v. American Civil Liberties Union, *supra*, note 5.
[21] American Civil Liberties Association v. Reno, 31 F. Supp.2d 473 (E.D. Pa., 1999), *aff'd*, 217 F.3d 162 (3d Cir. 2000), *vacated and remanded sub nom.* Ashcroft v. American Civil Liberties Union, 535 U.S. 564 (2002), *aff'd on remand*,322 F.3d 240 (3d Cir. 2003).
[22] *Reno, supra* note 5, at 874.
[23] P.L. 106-554 incorporated H.R. 5666, 106 th Congress, Title 17 of which is CIPA.
[24] United States v. American Library Association, No. 02-316 (U.S., June 23, 2003).

Index

abuse, 24, 80, 107, 108
Action for Children's Television, 5, 30, 35, 37, 38, 39, 40, 99
activities, 3, 4, 6, 7, 8, 9, 11, 12, 21, 31, 74, 81, 88, 91, 92, 98, 99, 109
administration, 84
advertising, 43
advocacy, 44, 55
age, 44, 50, 80, 81, 86, 95, 107, 109
aid, 50
assessment, 86, 95, 99
assets, 92
association, 64
authority, 4, 22, 25, 26, 27, 28, 78, 79, 95
benefits, 85
blasphemy, 10
broadcast media, 19, 21, 22, 23, 24, 25, 28, 38, 72, 98, 99, 109, 112
broadcast television industry, 44, 55
business, 62, 64, 65, 74, 79, 83, 110
cable service, 78, 79, 80
cable system, 76
cable television, 19, 23, 24, 28, 36, 37, 76, 77, 78, 79, 80, 99, 109, 112
Cable Television Consumer Protection and Competition Act of 1992, 77
California, 29, 35, 36, 38, 62, 71, 73, 94, 97, 112
channels, 19, 23, 24, 36, 37, 77, 78, 79, 80, 94, 100
character, 15, 70, 71, 73
children, 4, 5, 7, 8, 13, 15, 17, 18, 19, 21, 22, 24, 25, 27, 28, 30, 37, 39, 41, 42, 43, 44, 46, 47, 48, 49, 50, 51, 52, 53, 54, 56, 59, 69, 72, 77, 78, 79, 82, 85, 93, 95, 98, 101, 107, 108
Clear Channel Broadcasting, 13, 34
Clinton, 43, 82
Columbia, 5, 24, 29, 69, 72
commercial, 38, 63, 64, 67, 80, 82, 83, 86, 87, 110, 112
Communications Act of 1934, 41, 53, 68, 76, 78, 98, 103
Communications Decency Act, 35, 36, 60, 78, 80, 100, 106, 109
communities, 85, 86, 107
community, 4, 6, 10, 11, 21, 44, 55, 61, 62, 73, 81, 83, 85, 86, 91, 94, 98, 99, 102, 103, 104, 106, 109, 110, 111
compliance, 12, 13, 68
computers, 60, 87, 111
congress, iv, 1, 2, 3, 5, 6, 14, 15, 16, 17, 18, 20, 27, 37, 39, 41, 42, 43, 46, 47, 48, 49, 51, 52, 54, 55, 59, 60, 61, 69, 71, 72, 79, 82, 84, 88, 89, 93, 95, 99, 105, 107, 108, 113
Congress, iv, 1, 2, 3, 5, 6, 14, 15, 16, 17, 18, 20, 27, 37, 39, 41, 42, 43, 46, 47, 48, 49, 51, 52, 54, 59, 60, 61, 69, 71, 72, 79, 82, 84, 88, 89, 93, 95, 99, 105, 107, 108, 113
consent, 12, 13
Constitution, 36, 60, 68, 76, 78
consumers, 42, 46
content, 3, 18, 19, 20, 24, 25, 36, 37, 42, 43, 44, 47, 49, 50, 51, 52, 54, 59, 61, 63, 68, 79, 80, 82, 84, 86, 87, 93, 95, 102, 103, 108
Conversion, 57

Copyright, iv
costs, 87, 111
credit, 83, 110
crime, 60, 63, 64, 65, 70, 73, 74, 76, 80, 81, 84, 90, 91
cultural, vii
culture, 65
customers, 64, 73, 79
Customs Service, 93
cyberspace, 35
danger, 23, 61
demand, 67
development, 39, 52, 53
Development, 43
Direct Broadcast Satellite, 96
direct costs, 87, 111
drugs [medicines], 13
drugs [narcotics], 13
education, 9
Education, 103
election, 89
e-mail, 60, 109
employees, 13
English, 10
family, 50, 63
Family, 49, 50, 52, 53, 56
Federal Communications Commission, vii, 2, 4, 5, 9, 17, 18, 19, 28, 30, 38, 41, 49, 54, 62, 70, 71, 77, 90, 94, 95, 98, 99, 112
Federal Communications Commission (FCC), vii, 1, 2, 3, 4, 5, 6, 7, 8, 9, 10, 12, 14, 15, 16, 17, 18, 19, 20, 21, 22, 23, 24, 25, 28, 29, 30, 34, 35, 37, 38, 39, 40, 41, 42, 43, 44, 46, 47, 48, 49, 52, 53, 54, 56, 57, 62, 70, 71, 72, 77, 90, 94, 95, 98, 99, 112
female, 3, 71, 83, 103, 110
females, 107
films, 62, 63, 64, 91
First Amendment, 2, 6, 11, 19, 20, 21, 22, 23, 24, 25, 26, 27, 28, 36, 38, 43, 59, 61, 62, 63, 64, 65, 66, 67, 69, 71, 72, 73, 77, 79, 81, 85, 86, 88, 89, 91, 92, 93, 94, 97, 99, 104, 105, 107, 108, 109
foreign, 59, 60, 68, 69, 70, 73, 74, 76, 90
free, 5, 22, 100
freedom, 59, 61, 64, 85, 89, 105
funding, 52
funds, 60, 87, 88, 89, 103, 111
Georgia, 62, 94, 96
goals, 5, 84, 89
Golden Globe Awards, 1, 2, 3, 9, 10, 14, 16, 17, 29, 31, 32
Government, 23, 38, 39, 69, 70, 72, 73, 78, 79, 82, 86, 87, 101, 108
grants, 103
greed, 44
groups, 43, 51, 83
guilty, 92, 97, 100
high school, 9
history, 35, 54
Home Box Office, 44
House, 2, 14, 15, 16, 17, 35, 41, 46, 48, 54, 56
ideas, 20, 35
Illinois, 61, 95, 106
indecency, vii, 1, 2, 4, 5, 6, 9, 10, 11, 12, 13, 14, 15, 16, 17, 18, 28, 29, 30, 32, 33, 34, 35, 37, 39, 41, 46, 48, 54, 76, 77, 78, 80, 100, 105, 106, 110
Indian, 70
indicators, 45
industry, vii, 41, 43, 44, 46, 47, 55
Infinity Broadcasting, 12, 30, 33
Inflation, 31
Information, 98, 112
inspections, 64
institutions, 102
interest, 4, 17, 22, 23, 24, 25, 26, 27, 37, 38, 39, 61, 62, 65, 66, 67, 69, 70, 72, 73, 77, 79, 82, 83, 84, 85, 86, 88, 89, 94, 95, 98, 101, 106, 109, 112

Index

Internet, 19, 48, 50, 60, 82, 83, 84, 85, 86, 87, 88, 89, 90, 99, 102, 103, 106, 108, 111
Interval, 54
issues, 9, 23, 52, 62, 98, 106
jurisdiction, 70, 91, 104
justice, 88
language, 3, 4, 6, 8, 9, 10, 14, 16, 18, 19, 20, 21, 22, 25, 26, 27, 31, 38, 42, 44, 47, 54, 55, 57, 68, 71, 72, 76, 85, 98
laws, 13, 22, 54, 65, 94, 104
lawyers, 75
leadership, 44
learning, 104
legal, iv, 1, 2, 49, 95
legislation, 1, 2, 14, 15, 17, 18, 41, 46, 48, 52, 108
licenses, 23
limitation, 23, 63, 64
listening, 5, 13
male, 94
market, 16, 48
marketing, 47
measures, 18
media, vii, 16, 19, 21, 22, 23, 24, 25, 28, 38, 42, 43, 49, 50, 52, 54, 55, 71, 72, 79, 98, 99, 109, 112
minors, 5, 20, 22, 26, 27, 28, 38, 40, 48, 60, 62, 69, 72, 74, 83, 84, 85, 86, 87, 88, 90, 95, 100, 102, 103, 105, 107, 108, 109, 110, 111
Missouri, 38
monitoring, 41, 51
networks, 11, 16, 45, 54
nudity, 11, 64, 65, 66, 67, 80, 88, 94, 100
offensiveness, 7, 8, 62, 94, 106
organization, 18
ownership, 16, 23
Pacifica case, 4
parental authority, 79
parents, 5, 22, 24, 25, 26, 27, 28, 41, 42, 43, 45, 47, 49, 50, 51, 52, 53, 54, 56, 80, 85, 95, 101
participation, 11
Pennsylvania, 30
perceptions, 51
personality, 8
policies, 18, 48
policy, 17, 35, 65, 87, 90, 111
Policy, 49, 53, 56, 100
population, 49, 82
Powell, 3
power, 39, 60, 72, 76, 95
primary, 110
producers, 16, 54
production, 31, 44, 55, 67, 108
profanity, 8, 10, 32, 33, 54
profits, 60, 74, 75
public nuisance law, 4
public policy, 49
punishment, 92
qualifications, 15
questioning, 51
Racism, 96
radio, 4, 5, 6, 7, 8, 9, 12, 13, 18, 19, 20, 22, 23, 26, 28, 29, 37, 54, 60, 70, 71, 72, 95, 98
ratings, 30, 41, 42, 43, 44, 45, 46, 47, 48, 49, 50, 51, 52, 53, 54, 55
Reagan, President Ronald 42, 47, 56
regulation, 4, 19, 22, 23, 25, 26, 27, 28, 34, 35, 37, 65, 67, 77, 79, 85, 95, 97
Regulation, v, 1, 54, 55
regulations, 1, 2, 5, 6, 13, 17, 24, 28, 32, 46, 50, 62, 63, 64, 70, 72, 77, 93, 95, 99
relevance, 22
research, 42, 49, 51, 60, 87, 104, 111
responsibility, iv
retail, 63, 92
RICO, 60, 75, 90, 91, 92, 104

Index

risk, vii, 7, 27, 74, 99
Scarcity, 23
secondary, 64, 65, 66, 67, 97
Senate, 2, 15, 16, 17, 34, 41, 46, 47, 55, 56
sensitivity, 91
services, iv, 76, 78, 80, 87, 102, 107
sexual abuse, 107, 108
sexually-oriented programming, 78, 79
skits, 13
St. Louis, 38
staff, 10
standards, 4, 6, 10, 11, 21, 38, 44, 50, 61, 62, 73, 81, 83, 84, 85, 86, 91, 92, 95, 98, 99, 102, 103, 104, 106, 109, 110, 111
study, 15, 18, 47, 49, 50, 51, 52, 65
subscribers, 37, 79, 107
Super Bowl, vii, 1, 2, 3, 10, 11, 29, 33, 34, 46, 48
supervision, 5, 27, 72
Supreme Court, 4, 19, 20, 21, 24, 29, 38, 39, 59, 60, 61, 62, 63, 64, 65, 66, 68, 69, 70, 71, 75, 77, 79, 80, 81, 82, 83, 84, 85, 88, 91, 92, 93, 95, 98, 99, 101, 102, 103, 106, 108, 109, 110, 111, 112
Survey, 49, 53, 56
technical change, 17
technological developments, 24
technology, 44, 48, 53, 84, 87, 100, 108

telecommunications, 24, 60, 80, 81, 87, 101
Telecommunications Act, 5, 41, 42, 51, 53, 80
telephone, 60, 69, 70, 81, 98, 109
television, 1, 2, 5, 9, 13, 18, 19, 20, 22, 23, 24, 26, 27, 28, 29, 34, 36, 37, 41, 42, 43, 44, 46, 48, 49, 50, 51, 52, 53, 54, 55, 57, 60, 70, 72, 76, 77, 78, 79, 80, 98, 99, 109, 112
television stations, 2, 5, 34, 36, 54, 72
trade, 63, 83, 110
training, 13
transition, 53
transport, 59, 60, 73, 75
transportation, 70
US - 4, 5, 12, 13, 24, 33, 34, 35, 39, 41, 43, 54, 66, 69, 70, 74, 75, 76, 78, 88, 91, 92, 93, 94, 96, 97, 98, 99, 100, 104, 112, 113
values, 63, 65
video programming, 18, 43, 47, 78, 80
violence, 41, 44, 46, 48, 49, 50, 53
vision, 53, 57
warrants, 75
water, vii
websites, 52
White, 96
wholesale, 92
work, 43, 52, 59, 61, 106, 108